In Search
of the Highlands

In Search
of the Highlands
MAPPING THE CANADA-MAINE
BOUNDARY, 1839

The Journals of Featherstonhaugh and Mudge
August to November 1839

**Edited and with an Introduction by
Alec McEwen**

Acadiensis Press
Fredericton, New Brunswick
1988

TO ANN, SHEILA AND LAURA

Typeset by Folster & Cummings, Fredericton, N.B.
Printed in Canada by Wilson Printing, Fredericton, N.B.
Cover design by Roland Robichaud Advertising Inc., Fredericton, N.B.

Grateful acknowledgements are made to Danielle Boivin for wordprocessing the text, to George Wood for drawing the two maps, to Sylvia Adams for helping decipher Featherstonhaugh's journals and to the New Brunswick Department of Tourism, Recreation and Heritage for its financial assistance.

Canadian Cataloguing in Publication Data

Featherstonhaugh, G. W. (George William), 1780-1866

In Search of the Highlands

(Sources in the History of Atlantic Canada ; 6)

Bibliography: p. 115
Includes index.

ISBN 0-919107-12-5 (bound)
ISBN 0-919107-13-3 (pbk.)

1. Maine Boundary Dispute.*   2. Featherstonhaugh, George William, 1780-1866 --Diaries. 3. Mudge, Richard Z. (Richard Zachariah), 1790-1854 -- Diaries.   4. Canada -- Boundaries -- Maine. 5. Maine -- Boundaries -- Canada.   6. Surveyors -- Canada -- Diaries.   I. Mudge, Richard Z. (Richard Zachariah), 1790-1854.   II. McEwen, Alec C.   III. Title   IV. Series.

FC182.F42 1988 974.1'103 C88-098544-5   69707
F1027.5.F42 1988

CONTENTS

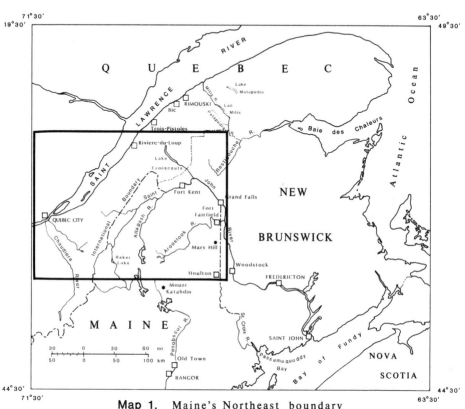

Map 1. Maine's Northeast boundary

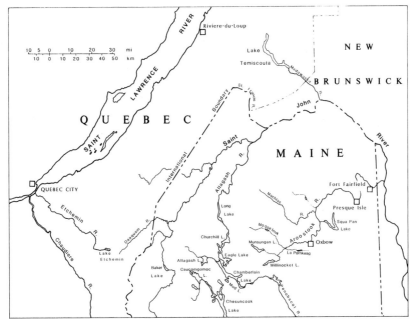

Map 2. The Featherstonhaugh - Mudge exploratory route in 1839

INTRODUCTION

The year was 1839. Britain and the United States were deadlocked in their controversy over the Maine boundary. The Aroostook War, a hitherto bloodless scuffle, threatened to become a major conflict unless the territorial argument was soon settled. In theory, this segment of the international boundary had been clearly defined in 1783 by a treaty that ended the Revolutionary War. But no sooner had the ink dried than difficulties arose concerning the meaning of the words. The eastern limit of the new United States was the St. Croix River, and the line ran due north from the source of that river to the highlands forming the watershed between the St. Lawrence River and the Atlantic Ocean. It then followed those highlands southwesterly to the head of the Connecticut River. The point where the North Line, as it was called, intersects the highlands was referred to in the treaty as the northwest angle of Nova Scotia, a province which until 1784 included the region now known as New Brunswick.

It took 15 years merely to identify the St. Croix, a name which in those days was neither in current use nor familiar to local inhabitants. In 1798 a joint British and American commission decided that the treaty river was in fact the Schoodic, and that the boundary followed the river from its mouth in Passamaquoddy Bay up to the confluence with its northern or Chiputneticook branch, and thence along that branch to its source at the place now called Monument Brook.[1]

The identity of the highlands proved to be even more elusive than that of the St. Croix. The United States claimed that the northwest angle was situated near the head of the Mitis River, a few miles south of the St. Lawrence, in a location that was thought to be comparatively low lying but was nevertheless on the watershed between the great river and the Baie des Chaleurs. Britain argued that the word *highlands* in the treaty necessarily meant mountains or a chain of elevated ridges, and that the true boundary went westward from Mars Hill, south of the Aroostook River. At stake were about 12,000 square miles of territory, much of it forested and unexplored. But in British eyes the actual quantity of land was not the most important issue. The United States demanded a boundary that came to within 20 miles of the St. Lawrence and, if adopted, it would hinder direct communication between Quebec and New Brunswick. The War of 1812 had demonstrated the need for a military road between the Maritime provinces and Lower Canada, but no such road existed. In winter, when the ice-bound St. Lawrence was impassable, the only convenient route was by way of the Saint John and Madawaska rivers to Lake Temiscouata, and then along the old Indian trail to Quebec City.

In 1816 a joint British-American commission was appointed under Article V of the Treaty of Ghent to survey and establish the international boundary from

---

1 Ronald and J.I. Tallman, "The Diplomatic Search for the St. Croix River, 1796-1798", *Acadiensis*, 1, 2 (Spring 1972), pp. 59-71.

the source of the St. Croix to the western extremity of Quebec at St-Régis. A survey of the North Line was undertaken in 1817 as far as the Saint John-Restigouche watershed, and in the following year the work was extended to the Mitis, but no agreement was reached concerning the location of the northwest angle. Since the commission could not come to a decision it disbanded in 1822, leaving the boundary settlement to the binding arbitration that the treaty provided for in the event of disagreement.

In his arbitral award of January 1831, King William of the Netherlands offered a compromise solution in which the boundary would follow the North Line as far as the Saint John River and then run westward along the river to the St. Francis. Britain was willing to accept the award, as was President Jackson privately, but the opposition of Maine and Massachusetts proved too strong and the United States Senate refused ratification, partly on the grounds that the arbiter had exceeded his powers and partly because of a belief that the recent separation of Belgium from his former kingdom had altered the character of William's original appointment and made him a protégé of Britain.

During the next few years there were several unsuccessful attempts to form a joint commission that would settle the problem. In 1838 Maine sent commissioners to undertake its own survey, but they did little more than retrace the North Line that had been run 20 years earlier. Meanwhile, there was growing unrest in the disputed territory, notably in the Aroostook Valley where clashes between lumbermen and government officials led to violence and arrests but, fortunately, no loss of life. The Aroostook War ended in March 1839, when Sir John Harvey, lieutenant governor of New Brunswick, and Major-General Winfield Scott, a special emissary of the United States, agreed that until such time as the boundary question was settled, New Brunswick would retain the Madawaska settlements and Maine the Aroostook Valley, in exclusive jurisdiction and without military intervention from either side. In the aftermath of this agreement, and because it wanted more topographical information concerning the border area, the British government decided to send its own commissioners to survey and explore the highlands.

On 9 July 1839 Lord Palmerston, the British foreign secretary, instructed George William Featherstonhaugh and Lieutenant-Colonel Richard Zachariah Mudge, R.E. as joint commissioners to report which of the following three lines presented the best defined continuity of highlands: the line claimed by the British commissioners of 1816-22 from the source of the Chaudière River to Mars Hill; the line from the source of the Chaudière to the point at which a line drawn from that source to the western extremity of the Baie des Chaleurs intersects the North Line;[2] or the line claimed by the Americans from the source of the Chaudière to the point near the Mitis River at which they made the North Line end. In addition, the commissioners were required to report to what extent the country at the northern extremity of the lines "claimed by Great Britain and the United States respectively, can be designated as Highlands in the ordinary sense of the term,

---

2 This line, lying between the British and American claims, was proposed by Charles Buller in 1839 in an article that appeared in the *Westminster Review*, June 1840. Buller was chief secretary to Lord Durham.

assuming that term to mean, as stated in the dictionaries, 'an elevated or mountainous region', and not a single ridge of hills". They were also instructed to collect whatever information they might be able to obtain "as to the former boundary between the old French colonies and the British colonies, before the year 1783, and as to the present Boundary between New Brunswick and Lower Canada" and to return to England when they had completed their operations "to give such verbal information and explanations as Her Majesty's Government may wish to receive".[3]

Richard Mudge seemed a fairly obvious choice for the task.[4] Born 6 September 1790, he served in the Peninsular War and later joined the Ordnance Survey where the director, his father Major-General William Mudge, placed him in charge of the drawing office at the Tower of London for several years. An accomplished survey astronomer, Richard Mudge was elected a Fellow of the Royal Society in 1823. He had considerable experience as a field surveyor in England, although a recent official history of the Ordnance Survey describes him as "not a particularly strong or effective officer".[5] In 1837 Mudge inherited a property at Beechwood, Devon. Like Featherstonhaugh he was attracted by railways, and in that same year he published a work in support of a national rail system.[6] Although a man of undoubted professional ability, Mudge was apparently more than willing to leave the conduct and progress of the expedition to his energetic colleague. Mudge's diary reveals him to be a genial, humorous man who very much missed the comfort of his family surroundings. His keen interest in fishing and hunting almost suggests a picture of a country squire enjoying a weekend's pursuit of birds and animals on the estate. More restrained than Featherstonhaugh in disclosing his true feelings to a diary, Mudge can hardly have failed to be aware of the lack of respect, sometimes amounting to contempt, that his fellow commissioner held for him.

Why was George Featherstonhaugh, an elderly expatriate Englishman, selected for the survey?[7] Not only had he left his native country more than three decades earlier, but he had been recently employed for several years by the United States government. The short answer is that he was an experienced geologist, familiar with North America. He was also one of the more remarkable men of his day. Born in London in 1780, the product of a classical education, and proficient

---

3 See Appendix.

4 The principal biographical sources for Mudge are Sir Leslie Stephen and Sir Sidney Lee, eds., *The Dictionary of National Biography* (London, 1921-2), XIII, pp.1152-3 and S.R. Flint, *Mudge Memoirs* (Truro, England, 1883).

5 W.A. Seymour, ed., *A History of the Ordnance Survey* (Folkestone, 1980), p.102.

6 Richard Z. Mudge, *Observations on Railways, with reference to utility, profit, and the obvious necessity for a national system* (London, 1837).

7 Biographical material for Featherstonhaugh is taken mainly from J.D. Featherstonhaugh, "Memoir of G.W. Featherstonhaugh", *The American Geologist*, 3, 4 (April 1889), pp. 216-23; W.H.G. Armytage, "G.W. Featherstonhaugh, F.R.S. 1780-1866, Anglo-American Scientist", *Notes and Records of the Royal Society of London*, 11, 2 (March 1955), pp. 228-35; William E. Lass, "Introduction to the Reprint Edition", *A Canoe Voyage up the Minnay Sotor*, by George W. Featherstonhaugh (St. Paul, 1970).

in languages and music, the young Featherstonhaugh moved in 1808 to Duanesburg, New York where he became a farmer and stock breeder. Fascinated by the emergence of steam locomotion, he co-founded the Mohawk and Hudson Railroad, the first successful passenger railway in the United States. Following a series of domestic misfortunes, Featherstonhaugh moved to Philadelphia where, among other intellectual pursuits, he published two books: a translation from Cicero and a mediaeval drama.[8]

While in Philadelphia, Featherstonhaugh delivered public lectures on geology and established a monthly journal to inform American readers about this revolutionary new science. His work soon attracted the attention of a federal government eager to explore and expand its national frontiers. In 1834 Featherstonhaugh was appointed the first United States geologist, and during the next few years he undertook extensive investigations throughout the mid-western and southern parts of the country. His highly entertaining and informative accounts of these journeys display a keen sense of humour and perceptive observations of his fellow creatures. But his urbane, disdainful manner, and his obsessive disapproval of alcohol and tobacco, did not endear him to many ordinary Americans. Nor did the fastidious aristocrat, who always carried two toothbrushes on his field trips and who complained constantly about the poor food and rough manners that he encountered, fit easily into pioneer surroundings. Americans, however, had come to accept the accomplished, eccentric Englishman as one of their own. After all, he had lived among them for 30 years. He had twice married into local society, and all his children were born in his adopted country.[9] His appointment as British boundary commissioner in 1839 came as a shock to the United States authorities. He was now seen as a viper that America had clutched to its bosom. Daniel Webster dismissed Featherstonhaugh, with typical scorn, as being "shallow and conceited, with quite a lurch toward mischief".[10] Such remarks were sour grapes, for the loss to Britain of an influential geologist was a blow to American pride.

A visit to Quebec in October 1838 seems to have paved the way for Featherstonhaugh's appointment as British boundary commissioner. There he became the confidant of Lord Durham, the governor general, and his powerful private secretaries, the brothers Charles and Arthur Buller. Following further discussions of the boundary question with Henry S. Fox, the British minister in Washington, Featherstonhaugh sailed in February 1839 for England where, two months later, Lord Palmerston offered him employment at £1200 a year until such time as the boundary commission was appointed, and thereafter a salary "in proportion to the dignity of the office".[11]

8 G.W. Featherstonhaugh, *The Republic of Cicero* (New York, 1829) and *The Death of Ugolino* (Philadelphia, 1830).

9 Featherstonhaugh's first wife, by whom he had two surviving sons, died in 1828. In 1831 he married Charlotte Carter, a half-niece of Robert E. Lee. Three children of the second marriage survived infancy.

10 George T. Curtis, *Life of Daniel Webster* (New York, 1870), II, p. 170.

11 Featherstonhaugh's diary, 30 April 1839, Microfilm 349, Roll 10, Vol. 9, Minnesota Historical Society Research Center, St. Paul.

Fortunately both Mudge and Featherstonhaugh kept journals of their experiences. Mudge's journal was published in Stamford R. Flint's *Mudge Memoirs* (Truro, England, 1883), which has long been out of print and is little known in Canada. Unfortunately it is not clear what happened to the original journals, which were probably part of a family collection since Flint was a grandson of Mudge, and the selection which follows was therefore drawn from Flint's book. Featherstonhaugh's journal was never published but forms part of a much larger collection of his papers, which were microfilmed by the Minnesota Historical Society in 1977 and the originals presented to the Albany Institute of History and Art in New York State in 1978. This material is available on microfilm from the Minnesota Historical Society, Research Center, 1500 Mississippi Street, St. Paul and I am grateful to them for permission to print the sections that follow, which are drawn from the Featherstonhaugh, George William and Family Papers, Microfilm 349, Roll 10: vol. 10 (13 May to 27 August 1839), vol. 11 (28 August to 10 September 1839), vol. 12 (11 September to 7 October 1839) and vol. 13 (8 October to 16 November 1839). The place-names used in the journals have been brought up to date by adding the modern name in parentheses. Where Featherstonhaugh left spaces that were intended for the later addition of names or other data, his unfilled blanks are indicated. The omission of the few words and phrases that could not be deciphered from his journal is shown by ellipses. I am grateful to David Bell of the Faculty of Law at the University of New Brunswick for supplying me with biographical information about a number of people mentioned in the text whom I was unable to identify.

On 12 July 1839, Featherstonhaugh and Mudge sailed from Portsmouth on the *British Queen*, taking with them their respective personal servants, Parsons and Thomas, as well as three non-commissioned officers of the Royal Engineers: Second-corporal Robert Hearnden, and Lance-corporals John McQueen and William McGregor. Upon their arrival in New York they were met by Featherstonhaugh's son James, an engineer, whom the commissioners engaged as their secretary and draughtsman at the rate of £300 a year. From New York the commissioners proceeded via Boston to Bangor where they arrived on August 7th. Featherstonhaugh's journal continues the journey on the following day.

PART ONE

FEATHERSTONHAUGH'S JOURNAL

8 August to 16 November 1839

George William Featherstonhaugh (1780-1866)
from *The American Geologist* vol.3, no. 4, April, 1889

Thursday, August 8th. Rose at 3 a.m., and between 4 and 5 got our party all assembled and put into an extra stage-coach and pair, and off for the Saint John River. Breakfasted at an indifferent tavern *à l'Américain*. The road is much better than I expected to find it and indeed it is a good, wide, well kept up road. Our route is about 120 miles to Houlton, in the vicinity of the disputed territory. Crossed the Passadumkeag, keeping the agreeable Penobscot always on our left as far as the Mattawamkeag, near where it empties into the Penobscot. Here we supped amidst a ferocious set of men, the most ill-mannered ruffians imaginable. The women were humane and attentive, as women almost always are. Our travelling companion, Mr. Tancred, is already cured of his admiration of the free Americans; no ruffians can be more free than they are, to be sure. Our night ride to Houlton through the wilderness was a horrid one. The roads were cut up by the American waggons, artillery, etc. when they were lately in the heroics. A hundred times we were near upsetting. Once we had to get out to save ourselves. If we had upset we must have remained there all night in the mud, as it would have been impossible to have re-arranged our luggage in the dark.

Friday, August 9th. Happily we got out of the bad road by sunrise and reached Houlton, a pleasant limestone country. A neat American cantonment on the hill, commanded as I heard by a Major Kirby.[1] The U.S. flag was there flying. Reached Woodstock in the Province of New Brunswick about 9 a.m. A miserable tavern, the people just like the Yankees in their manners, as all frontier people must be like each other! Got our luggage shifted into other conveyances, and in another cumbrous stage-coach started for Fredericton, keeping the right bank of the River Saint John for some distance, then crossing in a scow and riding thirty miles on the left bank. Dined at a miserable tavern *à l'Américain*, went a short distance in a very heavy rain, then re-crossed in another scow, and at length about 10 p.m. reached Fredericton on the right bank. The sentinel stopped us in passing the Government House, and Col. Mudge and myself went in, having at Woodstock received a letter from Sir John Harvey inviting us to stay at his house.[2] We had a short interview with him and promised to return tomorrow. Stopped for the night at Jackson's Hotel, a second-rate place. Got beds and retired as quick as possible, being excessively fatigued.

Saturday, August 10th. Rose before 7 a.m. Our baggage cart not arrived. Came at 8, everything wet through. Fortunately my luggage was all water proof. Most of Mr. Tancred's things wet through. Particularly glad that his snuff got mixed with his clothes, and wish the last feed of tobacco was in my power that I might destroy it. After parting went to Government House, found the family at breakfast. Sir John Harvey received me very kindly. I found an excellent bedroom prepared for me. After breakfast he sent for Chief Justice Chipman[3] and

---

1 Brevet Major Reynold M. Kirby, commanding three companies of the U.S. First Artillery Regiment, Hancock Barracks.

2 Sir John Harvey (1778-1852), lieutenant governor of New Brunswick, 1837-1841.

3 Ward Chipman (1787-1851), chief justice of New Brunswick, 1834-1850, prominently involved in the boundary negotiations as agent to the government and author of *Remarks upon the disputed*

Mr. Odell,[4] and in Sir John's Council room we had a long conversation over the maps. It was a great comfort to me, after my exposition to these gentlemen of the particular views I entertained in relation to the boundary line, to find them all concur in their opinion that my views were quite new and of the first importance. Mr. Chipman and Mr. Odell declared before Sir John that if my views could be carried out, the British case would be triumphant. Sir John expressed his entire concurrence with them. Here we remain a few days to organize the party that is to execute these views, and get a little repose. Sir John is a perfect gentleman, full of intelligence, and Lady Harvey[5] and himself unite in their wish to show us we are welcome. In the evening, Chief Justice Chipman, Mr. Odell, Lt.-Col. Maxwell[6] of the 36th, and some other officers dined with us. It was a very handsome dinner and good wines, the claret excellent. I handed in Mrs. Tryon[7] and sat next to Sir John. After dinner we retired to the drawing room and passed the evening very agreeably. Retired to my comfortable room about eleven.

Sunday, August 11th. Rose a little after six and finished a long letter to Mr. Fox.[8] The breakfast went off very agreeably. At eleven got into the carriage with the ladies and Sir John and drove to a very neat church, with a well dressed congregation. The clergyman was Archdeacon [blank],[9] a very admirable reader. The service was well performed and the singing good. Afterwards returned some calls with Mr. Tancred. At dinner met the Chief Justice whom I like very much. His information is precise, various and clearly conveyed. Also some young officers. We passed a very cheerful evening. This is a very amiable family. Lady Harvey is depressed in spirits by the death of her eldest son.[10] Mrs. Tryon is an agreeable gentlewoman and the mother of a sweet little girl about the age of our Harry.[11] Sir John is a man cast in the happiest mould. Tall, handsome, and an excellent figure, he is as far as person goes, the very model of an English general. His pleasant, lively manners and his hospitable nature soon make one attached to him. At 1/2 past eleven we all retired.

Monday, August 12th. This morning we had another long conference with Sir John Harvey, Chief Justice Chipman and Mr. Odell, and they having adopted all

---

points of boundary under the fifth article of the Treaty of Ghent (Saint John, 1839).

4 William Franklin Odell (1774-1844), provincial secretary of New Brunswick from 1812 until his death. In 1818 he was appointed chief surveyor to the British commission investigating the New Brunswick-Maine boundary.

5 Elizabeth, daughter of Lord Lake.

6 Lieutenant-Colonel Archibald M. Maxwell, commanding officer, 36th regiment of foot.

7 Elizabeth Tryon, the Harveys' only daughter, wife of Captain Samuel Tryon.

8 Henry Stephen Fox (1791-1846), British minister at Washington.

9 George Coster (1794-1859), archdeacon of New Brunswick and rector of Fredericton.

10 Captain G.L. Harvey, 70th Regiment, died 22 February 1839.

11 Harry Featherstonhaugh (1838-1881), born in Philadelphia, the elder son of Featherstonhaugh and his second wife, Charlotte Carter.

my views, and encouraged us in the prosecution of them, we engaged a Mr. Wilkinson as our quartermaster and commissary to organize our party.[12] I am pleased with Mr. Wilkinson and think him competent to the duties he will be charged with. My son being indisposed,[13] I walked to his hotel before breakfast and found him much better. Played at billiards for the first time in ten years with Capt. Tryon at the private table of the Government house.[14] Several officers to dinner. Passed a pleasant evening.

Tuesday, August 13th. Excessively engaged all the morning making arrangements and writing despatches. Dined by invitation with Col. Maxwell and the officers of the 36th at the mess. My health was drunk twice, and I had to make a speech which was greatly applauded. Returned home past ten o'clock. Mr. Tancred left us this morning for Quebec.

Wednesday, August 14th. Very fine day. Occupied all the morning preparing Despatch No. 1 for Lord Palmerston, and advancing our other preparations for our departure. Two Mr. Robinsons dined with us today. Mr. W. and Mr. Frederick Robinson,[15] the first exceedingly resembles his brother Beverley at New York. Got to bed soon.

Thursday, August 15th. Busily engaged until 3 o'clock finishing my despatches, which went today by mail. Afterwards took a drive with Lady Harvey and Mrs. Tryon, both very agreeable women. Lady H. is a daughter of Lord Lake's, known by his Indian celebrity. Afterwards took a drive to the south end of the village and made some calls. Col. Maxwell with some other officers and Chief Justice Chipman dined with us. We had a very agreeable evening.

Friday, August 16th. Excessively engaged all day. Chief Justice Chipman called and spent an hour in my bedroom, in company with Sir John Harvey, discussing various matters. Before dinner played a few games at billiards with Sir John. Dressed and at 1/2 past six drove to Mr. Odell's, Secretary of the Province. A large dinner party. The first N. Brunswick ladies I have seen. Mrs. Bailly[16] and Miss Odell, his daughter. Spent a pleasant day. Came home 1/2 past ten.

---

12 John Wilkinson (1804-1871), surveyor and draughtsman, New Brunswick crown lands department. In 1859 he published the first official map of New Brunswick.

13 James Duane Featherstonhaugh (1815-1899), born at Duanesburg, New York, the younger son of Featherstonhaugh and his first wife, Sara Duane.

14 Samuel Tryon, aide-de-camp and son-in-law of Sir John Harvey.

15 William Henry Robinson (1795-1846), member of the Legislative Council; Frederick Philipse Robinson (1785-1877), member of the Executive Council.

16 Elizabeth Baillie, daughter of Odell and wife of Thomas Baillie, surveyor general of New Brunswick.

Saturday, August 17th. The weather is now delightful. Wrote a private letter to Lord Palmerston and continued to perfect the arrangements for our departure. Played a game at billiards before dinner. I begin to hope the singular weakness in the muscles of my thighs which commenced with my winter voyage to England last February, and which has annoyed me and often given me apprehensions in London, is rather abating. At dinner we had the Attorney General[17] and some other persons of the Province. Retired to bed at 10 p.m.

Sunday, August 18th. After breakfast dressed and went to church. Excessively hot. Passed the rest of the day until dinner in my room writing a long private letter to Lord Palmerston. No strangers to dinner, which was a great relief. My friend Sir John Caldwell[18] has rather crooked views about the boundary question, on account of his private interests.

Monday, August 19th. Beautiful day but very hot. News of the great fire in Saint John confirmed. One hundred and fifty houses, with a great number of ware-houses and stores burnt. Some reason to apprehend that our tents, stores, etc. preparing at Saint John are also burnt, which would be a very untoward occur-rence. I have therefore determined to run down to be on the spot, in order to prevent further delay. Sir John Harvey has determined on account of the magnitude of the calamity to go down himself so that we shall leave this place tomorrow morning. Had a pleasant dinner party, without any company. Went to bed early.

Tuesday, August 20th. Another charming day. At 7 a.m. Sir John Harvey, Capt. Tryon and myself embarked on the steamer for Saint John. This is a truly magnificent and beautiful river, far exceeding the Hudson in the grandeur of its dimensions, though not improved by villages and cultivation as that charming river is. When within about 25 miles of Saint John we entered the gorge of a fine range of highlands traversing the country from N.E. to S.W. This range appears to consist of stratified calcareous slate, the strike being from N.E. to S.W. I could only see the stratification from the boat. The range lasts all the way to Saint John and is occasionally interrupted. About 5 miles from Saint John passed that noble river the Kennebecasis, which comes in from E.N.E. Sir John says this is one of the finest parts of New Brunswick and that it is well settled, he having sailed up it 70 miles. Reached Saint John about 1/2 past 4 p.m. The Chief Justice and some members of the Corporation at the wharf at Indian town to receive the Lt. Governor. Drove 2 miles to the Saint John Hotel, passing through the burnt district, a bad looking affair. Dined at 1/2 past 6.

Wednesday, August 21st. A so-so sort of hotel, kept by Americans. This is a vulgar fishing town with a great many small stores. Some respectable merchants. The manners of the people resemble those of the low people in all American

---

17 Charles Jeffery Peters (1772-1848), the last attorney general of New Brunswick to hold office under a life appointment.

18 Sir John Caldwell (1775-1842), a former receiver-general of Lower Canada.

towns. The best emigrants always go to farms or into the U.S., whilst the low, drunken, poor vagabonds unable to get any further remain in the town they disembarked at. After breakfast received a great many visits from Major Brookes of the 69th foot, the mayor and other gentlemen. Called upon Chief Justice Chipman who resides in a good mansion house, agreeably situated with a fine view out to the Bay of Fundy. Walked to a cove on the east of town. The place is built on a calcareous slate, sometimes having broad seams of limestone. This appears to belong to the Cambrian Rocks of Sedgwick.[19] No fossils. The dip is to the S.E. and the strike N.E. & S.W. I see now into the geology of this country. Very much occupied all day studying the geology, with a view to my operations in the disputed territory and hastening my preparations.

At 1/2 past 6 p.m. Sir John and myself drove to the Chief Justice's for dinner, where found a pleasant party. Mrs. [Elizabeth] Chipman is a good looking pleasant matron, sat next to her at dinner. Capt. Stewart of the Navy there,[20] a nephew of Lord Anglesey's. Major Brookes I like very much. Sir John's young son Warwick being just arrived from England via Halifax, we bade the dinner party adieu and returned to our hotel. A Yankee fellow at 11 p.m. came to the room to ask Sir John to go upstairs and look at some paintings, stating before us all that he had had the room fitted up and lighted, when to oblige him we accompanied Sir John upstairs, where he had nothing but a wretched magic lantern. A more impudent and ignorant fellow I never saw. His name was Rogers.

Thursday, August 22nd. At 7 a.m. drove to the steamer. A heavy fog, which they say is a common thing at Saint John. Got rid of it in the river. Had a fine sail up the beautiful Saint John [to Fredericton] where arrived at 1/2 past 4 p.m. All the officers on the wharf to receive Sir John and his son Warwick, who had just obtained a commission in their regiment, the 36th. Drove to the comfortable Government House, where Lady Harvey was made happy by the arrival of her son. Col. Maxwell and Capt. Nugent[21] dined with us. Retired to my room very early.

Friday, August 23rd. Very busy today. The people whom we have engaged to forward our party and provisions are like all low people, arrant rogues, and endeavour to cheat and impose upon me at every step I take. Their extravagant demands, because I am disbursing for Government, are disgraceful, and give me a great deal of trouble which no-one shares with me. Got in late to dinner, harried and perplexed with the misconduct of all the people. Met Col. Mudge in a carriage going to a review of the 36th. After dinner had to go out again and make new arrangements. At 10 at night engaged another tow boat to take us and the instruments, giving the monstrous price of £5.0 per day, and one or two days to return. They are quite as bad as the people in the States.

---

19 Adam Sedgwick (1785-1873), English geologist who in 1836 gave the name Cambrian to the oldest fossiliferous rock strata.

20 Commander the Honourable Keith Stewart, R.N. (1814-79), captain of the *Ringdove*.

21 Captain Andrew Nugent, 36th Regiment.

Saturday, August 24th. Obliged to walk into town to look after the people of the boat. Fell down Sir John Harvey's steps last night when going out after dark to engage this last boat, and twisted the ankle of my right foot, which gives me a great deal of pain. Excessively worried in having constantly to go backwards and forwards. Breakfasted with the family. Although we were to be off at seven a.m. we did not get away until 3 p.m., when the boat reached the Government House and took our luggage in. Bade a very cordial adieu to our most kind hosts Sir John and Lady Harvey, Capt. Tryon and his wife, and embarked. Found our boat comfortable. A little cabin about 12 feet long and eight feet wide, built up in the centre with a roof, and secured all round with tarpaulins against bad weather, which we can lift up at the sides and see the country around. A pair of horses, exceedingly well managed, towed us along a stony beach at the rate of about 3 1/2 miles an hour, sometimes having to cast us off on account of the logs and other impediments accumulated on the shore. The slaty rocks all run due N.E. & S.W. through the country. The land does not seem to rise more than 250 feet from the river at any point. There are a great many flats and benches from which the river has retired in ancient times. An extensive bottom on the right bank about 10 miles from Fredericton has a small village called French Village, containing a few Indian families of mixed Canadian blood, with a small church. At 1/2 past nine p.m. reached a place on the left bank, crossed the ferry and walked a mile to Long's public house where made a hearty supper and went to bed.

Sunday, August 25th. Rose at 5 a.m., bit by the bugs. The people of the house are civil, but entertaining such people as they do we cannot expect much beyond civility. All the second-rate taverns of this continent are alike. There is always something to eat, and a bed to lie down on. Generally there is always civil treatment. But what you may always be sure of finding is dirt, bugs, fleas, and coarse familiar manners. Walked back, crossed the ferry, and at 6 a.m. started again in our boat, which we found much sweeter than the tavern. At 9 a.m. stopped at a house on the left bank opposite Bear Island, washed, shaved and breakfasted. Good fried salmon, boiled eggs and tea; cream and butter in abundance for a quarter of a dollar each, a very reasonable price.

The rocks here are a great breadth of pudding stone, bearing E.S.E. & W.N.W., varying from the common strike of the country. The land rises to 200 feet on each side of the river, sloping very gradually down to an occasional level, and thickly settled with farm houses. This is a fine grazing country. Some fields of wheat look well. I perceive also some patches of Indian corn, short stalks and backwards. Potatoes succeed admirably. A very hardy population will fill this country in time. The woods are dense and much filled up with evergreens. It is a very beautiful river.

About 9 miles further up the country the rocks change to granite of the porphyritic kind, large but irregular crystals of reddish felspar. This rock has a stratified appearance, is on its edges, the strike S.E. Here the country becomes mountainous in its character, the right bank becoming lofty and gradually assuming a ridge-like appearance. These hills are 500 to 700 feet high occasionally, well rounded at the top and covered with timber, principally evergreen; they come by a gentle slope to the river.

At 6 p.m. stopped for the night at Howe's, a civil person whose wife and daughter gave us a comfortable supper, treating us afterwards to the greatest abundance of bugs. We slept very little. Col. Mudge is beginning to taste the peculiarities of travelling amongst settlers in North America. He bears it good-naturedly. The country here is altogether granite and covered with immense boulders of a very beautiful grey and white kind, with various curious blotches of mica and narrow bands of quartz. The ridge is lofty here, bearing East of North. Immense quantities of little black flies and mosquitoes, the people sitting at their doors in the smoke to avoid them.

Monday, August 26th. Rose at 5 a.m. and glad to get into the open air. Walked about two miles to Fox's saw mill to our boat at the head of the rapids. A cool morning on the river. We are out of the granite, the old slate rocks come in again, crossing the river in a N.E. direction as before. At 9 a.m. stopped at Jones' to breakfast in Southampton. A well situated farm on a fine flat and slope opposite Eel River, which is on the right bank. Got a good country breakfast, the women coarse Irish but civil. This place said to be 12 miles from Woodstock. Got away a little after ten. The land on the right bank from hence to the North Line boundary with Maine said to be very good. People complain that Government exacts not only too high a price for land but that it gives poor people no credit for payment. It was observed to me that the country would settle much quicker if poor settlers had the privilege of discharging their land debts by labour at stated prices on the public roads. If it is advisable to settle these poor granite hills, that would be an encouragement to poor devils. Good settlers would not have such land as a gift.

Arrived at Woodstock a little past 3 p.m. Got our cases of instruments down to the boat. Mr. [Joseph Ayres Cunliffe] Phillips, the master of the boat, seems very desirous of our going no further tonight, and gives us no satisfactory reason except that we shall not be well accommodated beyond this. We, however, are determined to go as far as the Guisiguit [Brook]. At length he confesses that his family lives within a mile, and agrees to take us to the point we wish to arrive at, provided we will stay at Woodstock tonight. Finding it late we agree, and so sup at the Woodstock Hotel. Mr. English, the postmaster, called to talk with us, also a Capt. [John S.] Dwyer, an Irishman wearing mustachios. Capt. Tryon spoke of him to me as a curious person who wrote for the newspapers. He wants to accompany Col. Mudge and myself, but I don't fancy him. After bidding us goodbye, this whiskered person came familiarly back to my private parlour, sat himself down at the table, took up one of my books and began to read just as if he was at home. I gave him to perceive I wished to be alone, and he marched off to drink and talk with some persons boarding, like himself, at the tavern. Had a bed spread on the floor, and after reading an hour laid down.

Tuesday, August 27th. Kept awake by the noise of drunken persons and the bugs. Rose at 1/2 past 4 a.m., paid our bill, and in a hard rain drove in a small waggon two miles to our boat. James and the servants had to walk. Reached the boat cold and wet. A rainy day. The banks of the Saint John here are very beautiful. Elevated about 200 feet at the distance of a mile, they slope gently down to the river, leaving one or two graceful broad terraces from whence the river has retired in ancient times. These terraces, together with the banks of the river, are formed of gravel, sand and loam; they are evidently the ancient bottoms of the river. The traversing becomes occasionally difficult, the water sometimes deep enough to oblige the horses to swim, and sometimes the water is too shallow and we hit the bottom of our boat against the stones. The river is certainly very beautiful, and the land good. But for the rigour of the climate during winter, this country would be thickly settled, which it is not. We seem to have left the country of boulders, where it was so difficult to tow that we were obliged to have a man following the horses, to cast the tow rope off where a rock brought it up. Upon all these occasions I could not but admire the dexterity of both horses and rider, jumping over walls, canoes and everything they met with under their feet.

At eleven reached Mrs. Harvey's, a widow living on the right bank at Wakefield, 5 miles from Woodstock. Her husband, a citizen of Maine following the occupation of both farmer and lumberer, was drowned about two months ago by the upsetting of a canoe coming down with lumber. He has left her with two little girls. She very actively set to work and got us a good breakfast ready. At 1/4 past 12 got into the boat again in the rain, and proceeded up this beautiful stream. As this river contracts it becomes very picturesque, the benches or terraces, once the ancient bottom, are well defined, and make admirable levels for the river farms. Towards evening the weather began to clear up.

At 8 p.m. reached Mr. Carr's, a Scotchman married to a hardy little English-woman. Here we supped on good fresh salmon, tea, and bread and butter, and at 1/2 past 9 p.m. laid down on a bed on the floor. Nye, the American who has established himself on Fish River, came to the house and went away without asking to see us.

Wednesday, August 28th. Rose at 1/2 past 4 a.m., a beautiful clear morning. Got into the boat and started immediately. The river continues very attractive. High banks of diluvium, gravel and loam, 30 feet in some instances, evidently the old bed of the river. At 7 a.m. reached the Guisiguit, in the neighbourhood of which lives one Pomphret,[22] an old soldier married to a Fredericton woman who seems to have a touch of Indian blood in her. Her numerous children look very Indian. This man has a farm of 150 acres, rudely cultivated, does not own a horse, and is ignorant even of the names of the hills where he has lived twenty years.

After getting a homely breakfast, mounted some horses we had hired and started for Mars Hill, said to be five miles off, but which we found nearly double the distance. The last three miles we walked, on account of the approach to Mars Hill being boggy and on account of its very steep ascent. This hill is said to be 1500 ft. high. By the syphon barometer [and the mountain barometer] we registered [1,688 feet, 3 inches].[23]

It is well covered with timber: beech, birch, maple etc., with some hemlocks and spruce. Found slate in place in the lode at about 900 ft., and fragments of coarse greywacke strewed about, which probably came from the top. At the top,

---

22 Thomas Pomphrey, disbanded from the 104th Regiment.

23 This figure, left blank in the journal, is given by Featherstonhaugh and Mudge on p.10 of the appendix to their final report. The present height is 1,660 feet.

which we reached much fatigued, we found an ancient clearing and a scaffolding about 20 ft. high.[24] From hence we had a fine panoramic view of the country round. We saw and took the bearings of Mount Katahdin, the Bald Mountains, and a *long continuous chain* further to the North, occupying a great part of the horizon. Some smaller ridges were between us and three western heights to the North. I saw a continuous chain trending N.E. on the other side of the Tobique River. To the N.E. and exactly opposite the Pomphrets we saw Moose Mountain, a short spur running to the Northeast. The intervals between all these heights were, with the exception of a few third-rate eminences, a rather flat country, well wooded, the greater part being deciduous timber. To the N.W. the waters of the Aroostook take their source. I observed some water at one point to the N.W. Most horribly annoyed by the small black flies.

Mount Mars, or Mars Hill, is an outlier trending N.N.E. It is divided into three peaks and is not connected with any other ridges west of the Saint John. All these short ridges, including Mars Hill which is about a mile and a quarter long at the summit, seem to be truncated, worn away, and separated into fragments by some ancient action. Geologically speaking, this has not been difficult to do, the strata are not strong, slate and coarse greywacke. At the very summit of Mars Hill I found the beds of coarse wacke on their edges, trending due N.E. and called my son and Col. Mudge to witness the fact. There is a good deal of ironstone in this hill. I am now satisfied that all this country is an extension of the Allegheny Mountains, and I expect by and by to find all the fossils, the producta, spirifers, corallines etc. I having made our sketches and observations, came down the hill at 1/2 past 1 p.m. and reached old Pomphret's a little before four. Changed my clothes, and as soon as possible re-embarked and pursued our way to the River de Chute. At Pomphret's I saw a very pretty girl smoking a pipe, who said she had learnt to smoke at 7 years old, and that she now smoked from morn to night. Horrible custom!

The River de Chute, so named from a small cascade near its mouth, is not more than 2 1/2 miles from Pomphret's. The country here is underlaid by calcareous slate, much marbled with white carbonate of lime, resembling quartz at a distance. This in many places is an incoherent shale, easily disintegrated by water. I can easily account for the truncated state of the hills in this part of the continent, and which has its counterpart in so many portions of the U. States, in the Allegheny region. The extraordinary manner in which the country is covered with granite boulders at Howe's (vide Aug. 25) obliges us to look for a cause, and that cause was altogether equal to underwash the ridges which may have been once continuous, and disintegrating and removing the shales would thus create immense gaps in the ridges, leaving one short hill separated from another, just as Mars Hill is separated from Moose Mountain by the River Saint John. The lofty banks of the River de Chute show how this small stream has worn its way back through the slates, precisely in the manner the waters of the Niagara River have receded, washing out the shale that supports the superincumbent limestone. It appears to me that some extensively operating aqueous action has abraded and

---

24 Erected by Captain P. Yule, R.E. in 1836 for the purpose of obtaining a view of the distant country, during the survey of the proposed railway route from St. Andrews to Quebec. The railway project was abandoned in 1837, following objections by the United States government.

denuded the country, and that the rich bottoms of the Aroostook and other streams in the disputed territory are formed of the ruins of the calcareous rocks thus comminated. Slept at an American's named Giles at the River de Chute. We got a tolerable supper and were sent into a dirty garret to lie down on the floor, with the sky exposed through the rafters.

Thursday, August 29th. Rose at daybreak, very cold morning. Went about 15 miles to the Tobique settlement. Breakfasted at Tibbits' who keep house on a fine flat on the right bank of the Saint John.[25] Engaged one Sissons, an intelligent person, to take Col. Mudge, my son and myself to the Great Falls [Grand Falls], 25 miles in two one-horse waggons.

Left Tibbits' at 12 m., crossed the mouth of the Aroostook. Excessively annoyed by the black flies which have raised blisters all over my forehead and neck. We now commence rising a series of ridges separated by small valleys, the road running about a mile and a half from the River Saint John. The land at the top of the ridges is very good. Scarce anything but clean hardwood: birch, beech, maple etc. Wheat, barley, oats, clover, ferns, they all flourish here. This will be a fine farming country. I never saw a more promising one. The only drawback is the protracted and severe winter. This is compensated by continuous salubrity. All the rock from the Aroostook to the Grand Falls is limestone, blue with veins of white carbonate; the edges lie at about 60°, and the strike almost uniformly N.E. & S.W. I suppose it to be the equivalent of the Shenandoah limestone in Virginia. Nothing can be more certain than that we are upon an extension of the Allegheny ridges, and further to the Northwest I now confidently expect to see the usual fossils. The ridges I have crossed this afternoon all run N.E. and S.W., and I entertain a hope that they extend towards the ridges which separate the sources of the Saint John from those of the Penobscot. But I want more information.

At sunset reached the Great Falls. Drove to Sir John Caldwell's cottage; not finding him at home, walked down to the falls which are very picturesque, somewhat resembling those of the Chaudière, and about 70 feet high. They fall over the slate, alternately with a little limestone, which is of a very good quality. It is odd enough that no-one in this settlement, where there are about 150 people, knew there was any limestone. Sir John Caldwell's servant, in answer to my inquiry why they did not build chimneys in their houses, said "It's because we have neither brick nor lime, sir". Sir John, when he came in, told me he was glad there was lime, for they had told him there was not. The worthy baronet received us very kindly. It is now 32 years since I first visited him at the falls of the Chaudière, in company with Edward Ellice.[26] We supped and about 10 p.m. retired to rest. N.B. I learnt yesterday that Nye, the American who passed us at Carr's on the 27th without making himself known, when he arrived at Tobique in the night immediately proceeded up the Aroostook to the American Fort Fairfield, and returned early in the morning to catch the mail. Hopkins, an American who keeps a tavern at the mouth of the Aroostook, refused to entertain him and his party, and they

---

25 Benjamin Tibbits, at what is now Andover.

26 Edward Ellice (1781-1863), English politician and a deputy governor of the Hudson's Bay Company.

came to lodge at a loyal Scotchwoman's close by, who related this to me. Hopkins did this to save appearances. I have no doubt Nye's journey to Maine is occasioned by our arrival, and he probably went up the Aroostook to Fort Fairfield to concert some measure with the Americans there, perhaps to stop us. I hope when he sees Governor Fairfield[27] he will be satisfied he cannot do so with impunity. Hopkins, it is said, is going to be naturalised; he has got a good property in land and buildings and does not want to lose them. He is sometimes a very patriotic American, sometimes a loyal subject, and always I suppose an astute Yankee.

Friday, August 30th. A fine morning, reposed well last night. After breakfast brought up my journal and affairs. Then walked out to survey the place. The River Saint John contracts as it approaches the falls, having to wear its way back through a lofty ridge bearing N.E. & S.W., consisting of stratified blue limestone and argillaceous slate, frequently alternating with each other. The gorge on approaching the falls is very narrow, in some places not more than [blank] feet.

Here the rapidity of the water in its descent is very great, rushing down in foaming sheets. Perhaps the descent from the bed on the North side to that on the South side at the bottom is 150 feet. The perpendicular break is about half that distance, or 75 feet. This great fall of the river is made into a circular basin which the water has excavated. The general direction of the strata at this point is N.E. & S.W., occasionally varying and dipping about 60° where the strike is steady, but the beds here are very much contorted, sometimes assuming an anticlinal structure, and sometimes cut through at right angles. Whether this is done by trap or not I cannot tell, not having crossed the river yet, which I hope to do. The limestone appears to be argillaceous, for it does not burn well into lime. I have not seen any fossils in it yet.

I have suffered excessively from the black flies today; my face and neck are stung in every part, and so inflamed and swollen that I am feverish and nervous. These insects are so numerous that it is impossible to make an observation. If you stop for an instant to look at the compass they rush into your ears, eyes and nostrils, drawing blood at every stroke; every puncture produces an inflamed tubercle, a constant source of itching and irritation. My face presents the appearance of a person just recovering from the smallpox. The country people say they cannot live in the woods themselves when they abound as they do in this wet season. How we shall endure this torment I cannot imagine. I am afraid we shall break down under it unless a severe frost soon occurs to check these most horrible insects.

Our passage boat arrived today with the engineers and instruments. Mr. Maclauchlan,[28] the warden of the disputed territory, does not arrive, nor Mr. Hansard,[29] whom we sent to the governor of Maine. How few persons there are who know the value of time, or who are willing to make personal exertions in favour of a cause which is not immediately personally interesting to them. For

---

27 John Fairfield (1797-1847), governor of Maine, 1839-41 and 1841-3.

28 James A. Maclauchlan (1797-1865), soldier, surveyor, magistrate and road builder.

29 Hugh Josiah Hansard (c.1797-1853), a former inspector of New Brunswick roads, who was appointed to the 1839 survey by Sir John Harvey.

myself, I feel excessively anxious to proceed with the public business, but the people and the devilish flies combine against me. Came into an indifferent dinner, worried and inflamed, and almost out of temper. Went to bed before nine.

Saturday, August 31st. A very steady rainy day. My head swollen and inflamed with the flies. Got a good cup of tea and felt somewhat relieved after breakfast. Rain in torrents. I wish our provision tow boat was arrived, that we might be taking some measures for our departure. Mr. Maclauchlan will not stir this day. He ought to have come here as soon as he received my letter. Paid Phillips, the master of the tow boat which brought us here, and who returned today. Sir John Caldwell is very feverish about the boundary question. He entertains a high opinion of the value of his mill seats here, and I perceive that he fears a collision between the two countries will ruin his affairs here. This agitates him as all his estates are involved in his defalcation as Receiver General of Canada,[30] and his sole dependence is on this place. I perceive he would willingly sell this lease of the Great Falls which he holds of 21 years under Government, to either an American or English company, and the danger of losing the opportunity of doing so is what agitates him. Had some excellent fresh salmon to dinner, with good roast mutton. Went to bed very early.

Sunday, September 1st. Rose in the night and observed a fine aurora borealis. A low dark arch to the North, through which stars were visible, threw out from its edge fine rays and coruscations. A bright sky with stars showed that the rain had passed away. Rose at 7 a.m., a beautiful clear morning.

Made a hearty breakfast and walked out. The night having been cold and yesterday very rainy, I indulged the hope that those devils the black flies were at least enfeebled, but they are out again in great force.

Whilst Col. Mudge was preparing his instruments for observations of latitude and longitude, I walked out to study the cause of the Saint John River having made so great a bend here, and the following observations occur to me. The peninsula upon which the settlement of the Great Falls stands is entirely composed of detritus resting upon the compact slate and limestone forming here the substructure of the country. The lofty left bank opposite Sir John Caldwell's house and bearing N.W. from it is composed of the same detritus or diluvium. All this base matter has been brought here by water and deposited in an ancient channel of the river ready to receive it. I observed the same diluvial banks in various places betwixt the Great Falls and the town of Saint John, and have occasionally mentioned them as levels and terraces. We gather from this that there was an ancient bed of the Saint John precedent to the deposit of this detritus. This peninsula extends S.W. from Sir John's house about 1200 feet to a ravine, and since it is all filled up with diluvial matter, the rock in no place appearing much above the level of the river, it follows as a matter of course that the falls of the Saint John once occupied the whole width of this distance.

In my journal Aug. 25th I mentioned the immense quantity of granite boulders with which the country is literally covered, on Howe's farm and the

---

30 Caldwell was dismissed from office in 1823.

surrounding country. These boulders are not brought from a distance, but are torn from their beds on the spot, and subsequently rounded. (N.B. This is literally the case with several granite hills of great elevation near Mt. Katahdin between 50 and 60 miles west of this place.) The causes which produced such violent abrasions here must have left indelible marks in other parts of the country where they were in action. We find those marks in the broken-down state and truncation of the ridges which once went continuously through this part of North America, in a direction from N.E. to S.W. or thereabouts. This most powerful diluvial action has broken up the continuity of these ridges, torn the strata from their resting places, comminated and deposited them in the beds of rivers, in the lakes, and even on the tops of the highest hills. This is most certainly the truth, for the detritus of which the peninsula and the banks of the Saint John here alluded to are composed is coarse greywacke, sandstone and shale, leaving casts of producta and other fossils, and the various mineral substances found in every portion of the Allegheny series. Wherever I find the detritus, I find it composed of fragments of this character. It is therefore evident to me that the diluvial banks of the river, and the peninsula, consist of the ruins of the old strata, which once were in continuous connection with what now remains of the chains or ridges, and that they were deposited by the diluvial cause which tore the granite boulders from their beds in the ancient channel of the Saint John and formed the bed or bottom of that river, until the water wore its way through this diluvial matter to the bed upon which it now flows.

Of the rocky dam once 1200 feet broad, all of which is now covered with diluvium, except the portion where the river now falls, I suppose the Great Falls to have been the lowest part, and the stream coming down from the [blank] on reaching the peninsula would necessarily turn to the lowest part to escape. But as the whole excavation of this second bed was probably effected by retrocession, as well as by its direct course, the combined causes could not fail of directing the stream to the lowest part. There is a ravine at the S.W. part of the peninsula; this seems to have been caused by recession of the waters when, the level being reduced, they ceased to pass over the peninsula. This has since increased by causes now in action.

Mr. Maclauchlan, the British warden of the disputed territory, arrived before dinner. I like his appearance and manner. He is sprightly, active and intelligent, seems to understand the present position of things well, and I foresee he will be useful to us.

Monday, September 2nd. Col. Mudge is occupied making observations with his instruments. I see that he is a slow man, but it is evident that our instruments will have a very subordinate part to play in our investigations. It will be altogether a search after ridges once connected, to be put together by geological reasoning. I think I shall be able to demonstrate my hypothesis in a perfect manner, but it will require to be strengthened by extensive investigations conducted with diligence and prudence by all engaged in them. The mail of today will probably bring Mr. Hansard with the letters we expect from the Governor of Maine. I look with anxiety for the arrival of Wilkinson with the provision boat and the men. If we can commence our investigations in two days, I entertain no apprehension but that we shall complete our investigations before the winter obliges us to retire.

Mr. Hansard arrived about 1 p.m., bringing a passport from Governor Fairfield of Maine, expressed in very friendly terms. I no longer entertain apprehensions of being interrupted, neither do I think after this that the Maine parties will be authorized to make any further encroachments until our results are submitted. I learn from Hansard that Governor Fairfield supposes we have been sent all the way from Downing Street merely to see that the Americans have told no lies about their claims, so that Ministers may be able to surrender the territory with some grace. He further said that the Federal Government was pledged to sustain Maine in her claims, and that no person would be elected to the coming Maine legislature who would not pledge himself to go all lengths to support the claim of Maine. The facts and reasons, therefore, to be offered by us are to have no weight. If collisions can be avoided until the Maine legislature adjourns, I think all will go well. I had a pleasant dinner and went to bed early.

Tuesday, September 3rd. Fine morning. Occupied arranging for the departure of the party about to proceed to the Baie des Chaleurs, and taking measures to organize the parties proceeding by water to the sources of the Allagash, and our personal party by the route of the Aroostook, I feel much encouraged to think that my views will be fully carried out. I omitted to note yesterday the receipt of a letter from my wife of Aug. 15th, with comfortable news of my dear children. Wrote to her under cover to Mr. Wilkinson. Excessively hot weather today. After dinner we all went out to admire a very rare and beautiful aurora borealis. The delicate and finely coloured rays went up from near the horizon to the zenith, where they united in the manner that an umbrella at the point unites all the sticks. This lasted for several hours. The whole appeared to have a horizontal motion, and the rays were most curiously evolved and widened from behind each other.

Wednesday, September 4th. Excessively hot day. A Col. [Charles] Jarvis, superintendent of Maine for the cutting of roads in the disputed territory, called. He is brother to Mr. Leonard Jarvis, once member of Congress and now Navy agent at Boston. A pleasant sensible man this Col. Jarvis and, like his brother, a cantankerous democrat. But he is a man of sense and a person one can talk to. He confided to me that he was to be a member of the next legislature in the State of Maine, and that it was the intention to pass a resolution in law to take possession of the whole disputed territory. During a long private conversation, I urged that it would be impossible for our results to be laid before the Queen's government, and so come through the proper channels to the cognizance of the Government of Maine, before their legislature would convene, and that the precipitate action he alluded to would throw everything into confusion, and put Maine manifestly in the wrong. He at length came over to my opinion, and before we parted he pledged himself, both generally and in his place in the legislature, to endeavour to keep back all legislative action on the subject until it has been considered by the two governments. I was pleased with Mr. Jarvis's manner and conversation, and thought the interview of sufficient importance to communicate it to Lord Palmerston, Mr. Fox and Sir John Harvey.

A fleet of canoes arrived today for our service, part of which we are going to send up the Tobique to the Baie des Chaleurs. In the evening another beautiful display of the northern lights, they had a great mobility. Suddenly a thin white gauzy flash would be shot up towards the zenith, and as instantly disappear. It resembles the action of flame when applied to gas. Went to bed early and fatigued.

Thursday, September 5th. Another hot day. Mail brought no letters. Sent despatch no. 3 by mail today. Col. Ashburnham arrived today from Fredericton. I saw him at Quebec last year at this time, with his regiment the Coldstream Guards. He was then famous as a magnetizer,[31] and performed some curious feats before Lord Durham and myself. He is on his way to Quebec. Exceedingly engaged preparing for the departure of Mr. Wightman who conducts our party to the Baie des Chaleurs.[32] The weather is cloudy and this evening we had no aurora borealis.

Friday, September 6th.[33] Rain during the night, and cool N.W. breeze this morning. Gave Mr. Wightman his instructions and despatched him on his mission.[34] We are now getting everything ready to enter the Aroostook, as well as for the supply party that is to bring us provisions up the Aroostook. A good deal embarrassed about procuring canoes, and indeed everything else that we want, for this place has no resources, and there is nothing I dread so much as omitting anything that may cause a failure of our mission. To succeed, we must have the sure means of subsistence within ourselves up to the 15th November, when I think the winter will drive us out of the country. The weather is changing to cold, and wind getting easterly. Barometer falling fast.

Saturday, September 7th. Very cold raw morning, East wind. Therm. 52° at 6 a.m., yesterday morning it was 72°. After breakfast Col. Ashburnham left us for Quebec. Wrote to Dom^k Daly[35] by him on the subject of the ancient jurisdiction of France before 1763, south of a line to be drawn S.W. from the western termination of the Baie des Chaleurs to the sources of the Chaudière. Requested him also to speak to Col. Bouchette[36] on the subject of his most

31 A hypnotist, employing the techniques of animal magnetism or mesmerism.

32 George Wightman was later described by Joseph Howe as a competent engineer "who rough in his manners though he be, self-taught though he be, is a Nova Scotian of whom we may be justly proud". Wightman was the author of a surveying textbook published in 1845, which contains some references to his work on the 1839 survey.

33 Mudge's 49th birthday, an event that went unrecorded in both journals.

34 Wightman and his party proceeded down the Saint John to the Tobique, and thence via Nictau Lake to the Baie des Chaleurs near the mouth of the Jacquet. He returned to Grand Falls to take his final barometric readings at the observatory on 14 November 1839.

35 Sir Dominick Daly (1798-1868), provincial secretary for Lower Canada.

36 Joseph Bouchette (1774-1841), surveyor general of Lower Canada. In 1817 he and John Johnson, surveyor general of Vermont, acting under the authority of Article 5 of the Treaty of Ghent, jointly established the North Line separating New Brunswick from Maine. This remains the international boundary from the source of the St. Croix River to the Saint John River.

extraordinary profile section of elevations from the monument at the source of the St. Croix to the Restigouche, a section which bears his name and professes to be made by "Barometrical observation", but which is entirely false, giving to the country three times the mean elevation it possesses. Saw Col. Ashburnham off in his birchbark canoe. Packed up all my things ready for our departure. Took a walk by the South side of the peninsula, and came up by the steep side by which the deals are sent down from the railway (built after Palmer's plan). The slate crops out the whole breadth of the peninsula at the level of the falls 70 feet, and is from thence to the top covered by the detritus. It is very evident that the Saint John at a very remote geological period went over this part of the peninsula where the slate crops out, and that the water has worn its way back from that line to where the falls now are. There has been a wide space or lake immediately North of the falls. I give a sketch of the locality. [Sketch appears here.]

Sunday, September 8th. Cold damp morning. After breakfast Sir John Caldwell, being in a nervous humour, came into my room with a report that a party of N. Brunswick lumberers had last night broken open Tibbits' store at the Tobique, taken 60 stand of arms deposited there by the warden, and had to the number of 50 or 60 persons attacked and burnt the American Fort Fairfield above the falls on the Aroostook. I examined the man who brought the report, and do not believe the story. Mr. Hansard is of my opinion. The others are agitated and credulous. I advised Mr. Maclauchlan, the warden, to go to Tobique and ascertain the truth. He seems a credulous person, although he did not appear alarmed. The mail tomorrow will bring us the truth.

Took the elevation of a hill S.W. one mile and a half from us; 245 feet by the syphon barometer. This, added to 371 feet elevation above the sea at our observatory, gives 616 feet for the Highlands. Col. Mudge has completed the observations made on Mars Hill, which gave 1,285 feet above Pomphret's barn. Wilkinson went down the river to Tobique with our squadron to cross the portage against our arrival.

The elevation of yesterday is thus made:	feet
By level from tide to the landing	177
To the foot of the Falls	45
Height of the Falls	74
Height of observatory above the Falls	75
Height of S.W. hill above observatory	245
	616

Succeeded in calming my friend Sir John Caldwell. He is a very nervous person and this boundary question is so connected with his affairs, everything he has depending upon it, that he is at times fearfully agitated. The dinner passed off pleasantly, and a little after eight I slipped off to bed, being now quite ready for our departure.

Monday, September 9th. Disagreeable rainy morning. Awaited the arrival of the mail. A letter from the warden informed me that it was true some vagabonds, including that fellow Dwyer, had made an attack on the Americans about 3 a.m.

on Sunday morning, but had all fled on receiving a single shot from the sentry. This is unpleasant news, to find our own people playing the scandalous part of the *mauvais sujets* of the U.S. on the Canadian frontier. Wrote to Sir John Harvey and Governor Fairfield to assure him of our indignation at this base attempt and, lest he should receive an exaggerated account of it, that it was conducted by a number of drunken, irresponsible vagabonds beyond all control. As he will receive my letter together with the official account of the party at his fort, I hope he will see it is quite unnecessary to make a fuss about it. I shall go immediately and see the commanding officer of the fort. Took leave of my friend Sir John Caldwell and went down to the landing with my servant Parsons and the old Indian, Peter Denny. Got into the canoe and committed ourselves to the Saint John. It rained all the day. The detritus of which the peninsula at the Great Falls is made, together with the banks above the falls, continuing down the river in the same manner at least 12 miles. The lake I spoke of above the falls has extended many miles below. Passed a very marked ridge stretching N.E. & S.W. on the S. side of the Salmon River, and soon came up with another which continues North of the Aroostook. Reached the Aroostook in 3 3/4 hours from leaving the Great Falls. Found our people encamped at its mouth. Waited till night when the mail cart arrived with Col. Mudge and my son James. I got into it and drove in the dark to Tobique. Went to Mr. Frank Tibbits' to lodge on the hill. Found Mr. Maclauchlan there. Got myself dried by the fire and some supper. A bed on the floor.

Tuesday, September 10th. After breakfast rode through the woods to Fort Fairfield, on the Aroostook River. Saw Capt. Parrott,[37] the American commander. He behaved like a man of sense. Said he had transmitted an account of facts, as they occurred, to the authorities of his State, but that he considered the affair too *ridiculous* to be taken seriously. He was well informed of the names of about 20 of the vagabonds who attempted to disturb, and had Dwyer's name on the list. Three of them had been there a few days before to reconnoitre. It appears that after seizing the arms, about 30, on Saturday night, they reached Fort Fairfield about 1/2 past 2 on Sunday morning, got within 30 yards of the pickets, and went to a log fire burning in the open field. A sentry there saw them and fired, upon which they all ran through some oats and wheat, like men bereft of their senses, tumbling over the logs and stumps in the dark, and unable to find the road. Two muskets and five bayonets, three hats, an axe, some shoes and even boots were found. They reached Tobique by daylight and replaced the arms they had brought back. The party, it appears, was composed of great blackguards, and had probably been got together by some fellows whose lumber had been seized by the Americans when they took possession of this part of the Aroostook. Capt. Parrott behaved with great kindness and offered his services in any way I wished. We shook hands and parted about noon, seeing their frugal dinner placed on the table.

Fort Fairfield is erected on a lofty knoll which commands the river; higher up is a block house to command a boom they built across the river. There is a beautiful amphitheatre of hills all around, and the scenery is very striking. The

---

37 Captain William Parrott who appears to have relinquished his command later the same month and returned to his home in Massachusetts.

ridges run N.E. & S.W. Some of my people had already arrived with their canoes. On our return met Mudge and James on foot in the woods, also three carts with our provisions and baggage. Paid our last accounts, and ordered the Indian, Peter Denny, to call me at daylight tomorrow, when I propose going to the Falls of the Aroostook and joining my party across the portage. Supped at Frank Tibbits'. A most lovely evening after our late bad weather.

Wednesday, September 11th. Entered the Aroostook at 9 a.m. Found the rapids very strong 1 1/2 miles up, the slate vertical running N.E. & S.W., sometimes contorted and anticlinal. The ridges here are evidently the same axis as at the Great Falls; this is proved by the falls of the Aroostook River to the North. Here the water falls about [blank] feet perpendicular, with a rapid of half a mile further up, a lofty ridge on each side and the strata bearing N.E. by E. The slate at the falls is crossed with quartz, as at the Great Falls. Walked round by the falls whilst the canoes were carried along the portage. Took a specimen of the rock. Reached camp at 1/2 past 12. Found Col. Mudge and James, and all well except an adventure of the Col.'s who has tumbled into a creek from a log, got drenched and spoiled our chronometer. Returned at 1 p.m. to the falls with a barometer to take the elevation of the ridge. Got up a stout ridge bearing about E.N.E., the apparent height of the one S.W. of the Great Falls. Took the altitude. On our return shot a partridge.

At 4 made a grand start with our squadron, passed Fort Fairfield and the boom, and at 1/2 past 5 p.m. taken by a heavy squall and thunder gust with rain from the N.W. Stopped at the cottages of some French Madawaskans whose husbands were at work on one of the Maine roads, a miserable dirty set. One mile further, encamped on the settlement of a Mr. Bishop, decent people, dried ourselves, got their kettle aboil, supped and went to our tent. Miss Dean at Mrs. Bishop's said she did not know whether the child she had in her was a boy or a girl. The bottoms of the Aroostook are fertile and beautiful. It is the climate alone is against this fine country.

Thursday, September 12th. Got a tolerable night's rest. Up at dawn, shaved, washed and dressed, and off at 1/2 past six, rather later than I hope it will be tomorrow. Fine morning. Passed a pretty island, the first. The banks of the Aroostook are very pretty and well-adapted for farmers: the old bed of the river is evident in the fine levels, no highlands to be seen from the river. Stopped about 1/2 past 8 at one Murphy's who has made some clearings upon which he has good grain. This place is 1/2 a mile N. from Little Madawaska, a stream that comes in on the left bank. Murphy says it is about 20 miles to Presque Isle, which will be a hard pull for us to reach. Stopped at Murphy's to breakfast. A cloudy morn.

Observed on leaving Murphy's that the left bank of the Aroostook was composed of detritus of the same character as that of the Great Falls, and that of the Saint John. We have been pursuing a course N.W., N.N.W. & N. ever since leaving Fort Fairfield. Three miles from Murphy's the course changes to W., having reached the North end of the peninsula. A small brook comes in opposite, on the left bank, called by the Indians Eequahcasis; one mile higher up is another brook called Eequahkec. Peter says the meaning of this word is Eequah/broken, crooked or bent, casis/little; and the other Eequah/broken, crooked or bent, kec/ great. The Americans call this last Caribou Creek, from having killed one of these animals there. In one mile the course alters to [blank]. The meaning of Eequah is island, and Eequahkec means great bend. From Eequahkec this course being S.W. into due South.

Went 2 miles and stopped to dine the people at a Trout Brook, which having the name I call [blank]. Whilst the men were dining I myself went up the stream which, although full of logs and boughs of dead timber, gave us an opportunity of catching a few small trout. A heavy shower from the N.W. On our return, instead of finding the men finished, they had scarcely begun. What ravenous appetites, especially the Madawaskans. One young fellow, who had been gormandizing more than an hour, kept eating dry biscuit, merely because it was before him. Finally, 1/4 before 3 p.m. before got them away. Half a mile from Eequahkec, and where the river has a due South course, saw bearing due South a ridge which I suppose to be the continuation of that at the Aroostook Falls. I hope it may so turn out, as it might, to cross the Presque Isle Creek.

The evidence of the destruction of the continuity of the ridge is found in the detritus deposited everywhere. Indeed, the whole level country where no ridges appear seems to have been a lake filled with this detritus. An almost total absence of animal life on the Aroostook. No settlement this afternoon. All wet through. About 3 miles from our dining station I saw part of a ridge on the right bank, and at 5 miles out the same ridge on the left bank. This I take to be a continuation of the ridge running S.W. from the Aroostook Falls. On arriving at Johnston's, 7 miles from the dining place, determined to camp there and take the observation of the ridge in the morning. We are at the base of the peninsula made by the Aroostook, the distance across is only 7 miles. The inhabitants have made a winter road along it; this road is on the ridge, and Mr. Field, a person who has a farm near Johnston's, told me it was the identical ridge of the Aroostook Falls of which we have taken the elevation the 11th. Thus far my hypothesis is made sure. Called at Mrs. Johnston's, her husband is from home. Her cottage is clean. She says the people of Maine have included them in their census, and that the inhabitants are so anxious to preserve their farms, but they do not like to make any observations which show a preference for another country. Camped in her meadow, had a nice fried trout and potatoes for supper, and laid down to rest. Mudge killed 3 partridge.

Friday, September 13th. Rose at daybreak and took Col. Mudge, James, Wilkinson & Hearnden to the top of the ridge. Took the altitude by barometer, a lofty hardwood ridge. W. got up a tree and brought me down some instructive observations. In the meantime I carved the name, or initials, of our Virgin Queen, V.R., in broad letters on a young beech which will not be fit to cut down there 30 years. This is her country and we must keep it for her. At nine came down cold and hungry. Made a hearty breakfast, and at 10 a.m. got into my canoe and started the squadron, our course W. At about 11 a.m. passed on our left a continuation of the last observed ridge, being then 1 1/2 miles from Presque Isle River, N. 70° W. At 20 m. to 12, course N. 20° W. Reached Presque Isle R. 10 m. before 12. Course from thence N. 20° W. Opposite Hooper's, course due North.

Crossed over to the left bank at 1/2 past 12 and went to the top of the hill. James took the height with bar. 373. Had a good view of the country, saw the broken fragmented state of the ancient ridges. Observed a long ridge bearing S. 61° W. and runnning S.S.W. to N.N.E., apparently being about 9 miles long. It lies near the Squa Pan Lake and is in the range with the Aroostook Falls ridge. It is about 1,000 feet high. I shall name this ridge or mountain after [blank]. I had observed before that the apparent flatness of the country from Mars Hill was deceptive, and here I perceived that low ridges ran in various parts of the country, uniting huge fragments of the ancient chains, most of them running N.E. & S.W. We also saw various other apparently isolated masses, the Quahkatsis another fragment bearing [blank], and some distant hills and peaks bearing N.N.W., which we take to be the Allagash Mountains.

Re-embarked at 1/2 past, in one mile came to some very pretty islands, called by the Indians...creek or place of many channels. Good settlements here. Course due North. Our people stopped to dine at Peter Bull's,[38] a New Brunswicker, 4 miles from Presque Isle. Bull says he is the son of a British officer and a New Brunswicker, and hopes to continue a British subject. Bought some butter, and dried myself here. Left Bull's 10 m. before 4. Left bank of the river a ridge of fine diluvium with pebbles, 20 feet high. 1/2 of a mile further a strong rapids at the turn of the curve, course now N. 70° W. 1/2 past 4 p.m. high banks of diluvium, 35 feet right bank. 20 m. to five, very low land, a small island on right bank. During the greater part of this day many settlers on the river, some back from it. Grain all too ripe almost. About 6 p.m. we stopped to encamp a little below a smart creek called Salmon Brook, pitched our tents in a pretty clearing made about 15 years ago, a meadow where two men were taking caring of, but no family with them. They leave the place, having secured the hay. Here we made a hearty supper and turned in at 9 p.m.

Saturday, September 14th. A very cold night, too cold to sleep towards morning. At 6 a.m. Fahr. 28°, a strong hoar frost on the grass. Having washed, took old Peter down the river with me a short distance to fish, but it was too cold. Peter says in hot weather the fish flock to the mouths of the cool brooks and are easily caught. I had observed before that when the rivers are warm in summer they go to the brooks. A beautiful morning, our people all cooking for breakfast. Our canoes are overloaded, and several of our men are obliged to walk. Owing to this circumstance, and to our repeated stoppings, we do not make more than 15 to 20 miles a day. A boat with 4 Americans passed our encampment at 6 a.m., going down the Aroostook. Left our camp 1/4 past 8, course due W. Bought a canoe of Mr. Beckwith for £3.5.0 a mile from our camp.

Landing, stopped at Courrier's old place, took some specimens from a broad vein of red hematite iron, rather kidney-shaped in places on removing the superficial lamina. In some parts of the bed the ore was compact.... The vein dips very much at the brow of the hill, about 75° to the East. Came away at 20 m. past 10. Came West to a fine wooded island and the banks of the river very beautiful; fine flat bottom for meadows, and gentle uplands with excellent soil. 5 1/2 miles from

---

38 Peter Duncan Bull (b.1791), son of the loyalist officer George Bull.

our last camp the course suddenly changes from West to South, and a lofty hill heaves on right. River with heavy conglomerate boulders, strong rapids.

1/2 past 12 stopped at the left bank, at a point where the course changes to West. Here the men dined whilst I crossed over with Mudge and the barometer to take the elevation of the ridge on the opposite shore.... At the top, obtained specimens of the rock [blank], with sulphuret of iron in crystals and then white flakes looking like arsenical pyrites. Wilkinson got up a tree whilst I carved V.R. on a beech. The tree on which he climbed was about 70 feet high. Says he had a fine view all around, saw Mt. Katahdin &c, and that we shall intersect another ridge in about 8 miles. Came down at 3 p.m. tired, and immediately started in my canoe to pursue our route. At 20 m. past 3 passed Beaver Brook, course S. 70° W. 1/4 before 5, course S. 35° W; 20 m. past 5, S. 70° W. 1/2 past 5 p.m. a ridge of coarse conglomerate crosses the river, rocks and a strong current, no appearance of a good camping place.

Landed in a swampy place, an old lumbering landing grown up with rubbish. About to pitch our camp in a very comfortless hole when, going a little higher up, found a tolerable place with plenty of fuel. After some labour got into a comfortable way and had our dinner at 8 p.m. Two of our men, for whom we had not room in the canoes, were obliged to walk, as they frequently have done before, and have not made their appearance. Sent a canoe for them with two men who returned late, reporting they had been down the river 3 miles without hearing or seeing them, although they had used every diligence to discover them. I feel anxious about them and ordered a canoe to be sent at break of day, with biscuit.

Sunday, September 15th. Got a comfortable night's rest and arose before six. The canoe sent for the men. I find the Canadians are better voyageurs than the people we employ. I always get off at break of day with Canadians and go a couple of hours to breakfast. These fellows will cook before they start and we can't get them off until 8 a.m. They thus lose an hour gaping, yawning and talking after they awaken before they do anything, whereas by starting at daybreak every man is hungry and works with diligence to get the kettle aboil. It is true the fogs at daybreak would prevent our forwarding with entire safety in so indifferent a navigation as the rapids of this river present, and prevent our making observations. One of the men, an Irishman, has threatened to leave us if I compel them to start before breakfast. I must make out as well as I can with them, the whole management of the party as well as the carrying on of the geographical observations having devolved upon me. About 1/2 past 7 a.m. the canoe returned with the two men; they had turned up Beaver Brook, believing it a part of the Aroostook forming an island and, night coming on, had laid down without their coats, food or fire. They were delighted to hear the voices of our canoe men, and we were pleased to get them back.

Left the encampment at 20 m. past 8, course W. High diluvial 30 feet on the right bank. Course more S. 1/2 past 9 a.m. passed on the left another pyrites ridge like that of yesterday. Course W. 1/4 before 10 a.m. course S. 60° W., a ridge in view, 2 miles distant. 20 min. past 10, course due W. Smooth river, ridge on our left, 400 feet high. High diluvial bank on our right 30 ft. At 11 reached the new road the Americans are cutting to Fish River. A log building on the left bank of diluvium. Course W. Landed on the left bank and looked at the road, 2 rods grubbed 12 feet. Saw 3 young men engaged in working the road and spoke to them. Found the bed N.E. running across the river, with impressions of plants.

We are now entering the fossiliferous country. The pyrite and rock we have been examining is a kind of greenstone trap. 1/2 past 11 passed Kepsikaluk, jammed with fallen trees, called Little Machias. The greenstone trap appears to terminate here, and the ridge of it seen from the American road runs N. 18° E. From Little Machias, course due S. Beautiful and rich land on the left bank and easily cleared. This is a lovely country but the long winters, the mosquitoes and the black flies reduce existence to the minimum of comfort. 10 m. past 12, opposite Dalton's, high banks of diluvium on the right bank. Dalton's on the left bank. Opposite Dalton's (a treble-refined conceited Yankee), thin shale with thicker limestone containing coal, plant fossils, producta. Found fine specimens of red porphyry conglomerate amidst the detritus. The conglomerate we have passed today is altered by the greenstone.

Passed two hours collecting coal, plants &c. There is no doubt a coal field near here. The men dined here; at 1/2 past 2 left and pursued our course. Passed the Great Machias (pronounced by the Indians Mechays), half a mile from Dalton's, 1/4 to 4 p.m. River very beautiful with a few islands, low and open woods, rich soil. A bend in the river at 4 p.m., course due East, then S. 70° East. Passed Horse Brook, the banks very low now for 3 miles. 1/2 past, course S. 45° E. Met five fellows in a canoe, the first rencontre we have had. Passed Squa Pan Brook, runs 12 miles up the country. A mile lower down passed another mouth of the Squa Pan. They come in on the right bank and have their source at a lake about 12 miles off. About 6 p.m. landed and camped in a rough meadow of one Bottridge's, on the left bank and 3 miles from the St. Croix River. The busy and cheerful hour of encamping has its charms, all seem interested in adding to the common comfort, stretching the tents, cutting and piling the wood, cooking the repast. I find Parsons an excellent servant, full of assiduity for my comfort.

Monday, September 16th. Had an excellent night's rest. Rainy morning and mild weather. Old Mr. Cowperthwaite, son of a refugee from N. Jersey, occupies the place we have camped on. He has a deed from Maine, signed by McIntire,[39] the Maine land agent, in Feb. 1839; a quit claim at 50 cents an acre, 3/4 of the amount to be paid in labour on the roads, the other 1/4 in money bearing annual interest. They are not to be called out to work until the question of the boundary is settled. The frost on Friday night killed his potato tops. He never knew the frost keep off so late before, usually it kills the tops about the 4th Sept.

Made a hearty breakfast, and at 1/2 past 8 got into my canoe. Course S. approaching the St. Croix; 3 m. from our encampment the course is S. 25° W. Right bank rises to 100 feet. Pretty country, river about 150 yards wide. At 1/2 past 9 stopped to examine some rocks on the right bank, about 1/4 of a mile from the St. Croix; limestone, the strata running S. 45° W. and very much altered by a trap dyke a little to the South, cutting it at right angles and disturbing the strata around.

---

39 Rufus McIntire, or McIntyre (1784-1866), lawyer and congressman.

I had previously protracted my N.E. and S.W. line from where we slept at Johnston's on the 12th to this very point, and here at the very point to which I had drawn my protraction I find the very ridge, the course, and the rock of the ridge of the falls of Aroostook. This is the triumph of geology! At St. Croix we stopped at a store on the left bank of Aroostook, kept by Taylor Webster & Co. One of our canoes was broke and would go no further. We here purchased a new bateau for $15 of a Mr. Pilsbury who lives in a dirty hovel close by, a regular set of low Yankees of the roughest kind.

Symptoms of mutiny amongst the men; Wilkinson as a clerk is a very useful man, but as a manager of our rough canoe men is very inefficient. He has little or no authority over them, and has permitted them so to use the pork that it is already necessary to put them on an allowance of 3/4 lbs a day. With some management I pacified them, bought a new barrel of pork, and after a good deal of trouble got off from the revolting scene at 1/2 past eleven. Course S., the Aroostook about 170 feet wide here, and the St. Croix about 80 feet. The average width of the Aroostook below about 90 yards. At 12 a strong current and huge boulders in the river. Stopped at 1 p.m. at a small brook on the left bank, which I call Greenstone Brook, from the quantity of G. trap stones there, to dine the men.

Started again at 1/2 past 2 p.m., course S. River about 150 feet wide and very lovely, strong current and rocky bed, boulders of conglomerate and G. stone. Great destruction of the old strata here. Took the elevation by barometer at St. Croix; stratified slate on the left bank with limestone, N.E. - S.W. 1/4 past 3 p.m. stopped at a ridge on the right bank to take the elevation by bar. Cut V.R. on a beech where we suspended the bar. Wilkinson, who climbed a tall tree, reports peaks and small ridges to the S.W. within a short distance. Got into our canoes at 1/2 past 4 p.m. and our course S. 45° W. Course changes to N. 70° W. A succession of rapids and dead water as we ascend the river, very low banks of spruce, cedar &c. We leave our ridge as we get more to the West, but hope soon to come up with it by the river's bending to the South. 20 m. past 5 p.m. course due N. Coarse conglomerate boulders in the bed of the river, with pebbles weighing 5 lbs. Great masses of many tons at 1/4 to 6. Course N. 30° W., rapids and boulders.

At 6 p.m. joined our men who, being in advance, had formed a clever encampment in a thick low wood on the left bank. Now working, setting the camp in order, collecting fuel, arranging our beds upon branches of spruce boughs, occupy all hands for a while until supper. Having made a hearty meal of some trout, chub, potatoes, biscuit and tea, served in the plainest manner, I laid down to sleep contentedly.

Tuesday, September 17th. Rose before six, had our fire replenished, dressed and washed. A fine morning; a good deal bit in the night by insects. Got a comfortable breakfast of fish, tea & biscuits, and at 1/2 past 8 a.m. left our camp. A foggy morning and warm, Fahr. 57°, and the maple and birch leaves a little changed. This will make a good farming country. Took observations by 4 barometers before leaving camp this morning. Course N. 70° W. The river continues to curve so that we have only made about half geogr. explored distance yesterday, and continue in the same way, amidst rapids and boulders of greenstone and conglomerate. 1/4 to 9, course S. 20° W. 1/4 past 9, course S., shallow water, drag the canoes. Strong rapids. Men work admirably, look picturesque in their red shirts, handling their poles so manfully and gracefully. 1/2 past 9, S. 50° W., dead water, cloudy. 20 m. to 10, course S., dead water 200 yards wide.

At 10 reached the Oxbow, course S. 50° E., a portage of 60 rods on the right. 20 m. past 10, course N. 20° E. We have for some time been going through a small lake or enlargement of the river. It is about 5 miles from this end of the Oxbow to our last encampment. 1/2 past 10, S. 50° W., very low country, continues dead lake water. 20 m. to 11 a.m., course W. At 11 a.m. passed the Amquateus coming in on the right bank, a small stream. 1/4 past 11, course N. 45° W. My clever old Indian, Peter Denny, whose facetious and kind temper is admirable, speaking of his temper, said "Me very cross, me very swear". 20 m. before 12, a ridge before us on our left. Continues still water, course W. A most beautiful island with the ridge in front, a very sweet scene.

At 12 stopped at a small gravel bar for the men to dine. Crossed over with James, and the men with the barometer and Wilkinson. Col. Mudge stayed below to fish. A lofty greenstone ridge; this ridge has cut through the limestone ridge which has been carried away, and its hardness has protected it. There is an entrance at the St. Croix a short distance back of this intersection by greenstone. Wilkinson climbed a tree but could get no view to the South. Whilst he was up I cut V.R. on a young beech. James having made the observations, descended the hill with the men, and I came down half an hour after, leaving Wilkinson to climb another tree.

Got into the canoe again at 3 p.m., course S. 70° W. 35 m. past 3 p.m., another lofty ridge about the height of the last. Course W. Fine afternoon after the rain of this morn. 1/4 to 4, shallow water and boulders again. Course due W. At 4 p.m. passed some rocks in the river, bearing N.E. & S.W. A little higher up, strong rapids and boulders. 20 m. past 4, bed of river full of large boulders. Fine scene, our 12 canoes struggling manfully against the rapids; their white poles glancing in the sun and men full of energy and animation, a really fine scene. 35 m. past 4 p.m., greenstone trap in place on the right bank, bearing about E. & W. At 20 m. to 5, Mooseleuk Mountains in sight, bearing N. 30° W. about 10 miles. Water smooth again. The ridge we saw last has encompassed us hitherto on our left hand, and is in sight astern.

At 5 p.m. reached a clearing on the right bank, made by Col. Webster who is a partner in the store at St. Croix. On the virgin soil of this rough clearing which is very fertile, he has sown all sorts of vegetable seeds, upon about two acres of soil: salad, turnips of 2 or 3 sorts, potatoes, carrots, parsnips, cabbages, peas, beans; all these we found flourishing in the best manner. A small log house and stable also were on the premises. In the log house was a chest of tea intended no doubt for the lumberers who are to winter here, for all this has been done with an eye to the main chance, but it has been well done and has succeeded perfectly. He has secured an abundance of vegetables for the winter, more than a hundred men could consume, without the trouble and expense of bringing them here. How he will like our men helping themselves is another matter, but I will pay him myself if an opportunity occurs and I hope it will.

A beautiful evening. Mr. Wilkinson reports from the second tree that he had an extensive and good topographical view of the country. From his position Mt. Katahdin bore S. 42 1/4 W., and Mars Hill South Peak S. 85 1/2 E. Assuming their position as laid down in the last maps to be correct, we are thus enabled to ascertain the ridge from which he observed the country, and it corresponds well with our calculations. All these sketches must be re-examined at Fredericton when we draw up our profiles and sketches. I think we are on a way to make our case perfectly, and to join the ridge we are now following up with the one Campbell observed and visited, turning off from the sources of the Chaudière. After a hearty supper, laid down to rest in the potato field. Mr. Wilkinson added that he could observe the ridge he was upon extended as far as the source of Penobscot at the Seboeis Lake, and that it ran about N.E. & S.W.

Wednesday, September 18th. Rose early, a cloudy morning. Labelled some specimens...examined the maps and made arrangements for our day's progress. We are, according to my computation, only a short distance from Lepampeek (the crooked rope), which the Americans have corrupted into La Pomfriqui [La Pomkeag], a word I was surprised to find in this part of the world, but the Dr. Jackson of Maine who so names it does not know French from Indian, I dare say. Took some potatoes from the field and left my card in the log house with the following note on the back, "The Commissioners' party have used eight bushels of potatoes from this field, and there being no-one to receive pay for them, I request Col. Webster to address a note to Mr. F. at Fredericton, naming the person to whom the money is to be paid, September 18, 1839."

Left camp at 1/2 past 8. Course S. 60° W., crooked channel. Took barometrical observations before our departure. Course soon becomes due W. At 9, course S. 25°W., still water. 20 m. past 9, course S. 65° W. 1/2 past 9, course S. 20° W. 36 m. past 9, course W. At 9 m. before 10 a.m., course W. 12 m. past 10, course N. 25° W. At 16 m. past 10, S. 80° W. 1/2 past 10, course W. At 25 m. before 11 a.m., came to the La Pomkeag, a small stream running in from the right bank, very narrow, not more than 15 feet wide, and crooked. Went up it a fair ride and returned; 1/4 before 11, course W. A great many small islands. 10 m. before 11, course S. Diluvial beds on right bank, the first seen for some time. Bog iron ore. Still good water. 4 m. to 11, course W. 2 m. before 11, N. 75° E. 4 m. past 11, S. 70° W., then S. 20° W., then due W. Our ridge in sight at 5 min. past 11. 1/4 past 11, course W. At 20 m. past 11, passed the Mooseleuk, a small stream coming in on the left bank. 25 m. past 11, course S., S.W. & S., very crooked stream. Our ridge in sight, distant 1 1/2 miles. Pretty stream, low banks. 1/2 past 11, course due E., then S. 20° E. 33 m. past 11, course S. 50° W. and parallel to the ridge. Some wild hay cut here by lumberers. 35 m. past, S. 80° W.; 12 m. to 12, S. 80° W. Peter says it is 15 miles from the Mooseleuk to the Munsungan. At 12, a few conglomerate boulders in the river which here is about 150 feet wide.

17 min. past 12, S. 60° W. Stopped to dine the men at 12. They arrived at 1/2 past 1. Rainy weather, sat in the canoe 2 hours in the rain. Left at 1/2 past 2. S. 60° W., then S. 20° E., then S. 60° W. At 3 p.m., S. 40° W. and ridge ahead. 1/4 past 3, N.80° W., then S. 30° E. 1/4 before 4 p.m., S. 70° W. 8 min. to 4, due

S., then N. 45° W., then N. At 4 p.m., due W., a reach of 1 1/2 miles. Then a reach of 1/2 mile W. 1/4 past 4 p.m., due S. 35 m. past 4, S. 60° W. 10 min. to 5, course W., shallow. 5 m. past 5, S.

The entries preceding were made in a violent rain which lasted all the day and the whole of the next night. I was obliged to put my head under my cloak to observe the compass and enter my memoranda. At 5 p.m. we reached the mouth of the Munsungan, coming in on the right hand as we proceed. This stream, whose course from its mouth is N. 50° W., is one of the forks of the Aroostook, the other is the Milnekak [Millinocket], whose course is S. by E. None of the party has been up this last, but as it seems to run with the ridge we are following, I thought it best to examine it to its source, which I propose doing, leaving Col. Mudge to fish. We encamped half an hour earlier on account of the violent rain, of the dense wilderness out of which our encampment was to be made, and of giving the men time to chop firewood. All this and the pitching of our tent was completed by dark, and at length we got a blazing fire up, our clothes a little dry, and some tea, ham and biscuit, when at 9 p.m. I laid down.

Thursday, September 19th. Rained all night, but on rising before six found the sky clearing again. Washed myself and dried my shoes and clothes well. Determined on taking a party of light canoes, with our tent and beds and something to eat, up the Millinocket. Thought it best Col. Mudge should accompany us, on account of our taking the tent away, to which he assented. About 1/2 past 7 a.m. commenced raining again. 10 min. past 9, left the camp during the rain, entered the Millinocket, a narrow but pretty wild stream full of rapids, bearing a little in the general a little E. of S. Crossed the axis of a ridge at 10 a.m. of conglomerate bearing N.E. & S.W. Passed a lumbering camp, spoke with two men, Webster's, who had never been up the Millinocket. Heavy rain. White pine growing on the banks. At 1/4 before 11, rain began to abate, entered a wild flat ... country with a ridge about 3 miles off. We are evidently near the summit level of the country. The maples here are very beautifully red. 10 m. before 11, wind shifts to N.W., hope for dry weather. At 11, saw the ridge before N.E. & S.W. 20 m. past 11, course West, which it has been for half an hour. 1/4 before 12, came to an insuperable jam, as it is called in the slang of lumberers, the whole breadth of the stream being obstructed by driftwood. Here my old Indian, Peter, and myself, being far in advance of the rest, were obliged to cut away the brushwood and break down the jam for a portage. Just as we were beginning to carry the things, my son James appeared with my canoe, and thus reinforced we got our canoe across. At 1/2 past 12, I was afloat again, and at that moment Col. M. and the rest came up. Course N. 70° W. Stream shallow, 40 feet wide and branching, the cedar boughs nearly meeting across. At 1 p.m. stopped to cut some dead cedars away which obstructed us, at a small reef of stratified limestone and slate, bearing due N.E. & S.W., being identically the rock at the Aroostook Falls. This is a remarkable coincidence, every opinion which I have expressed is now verified. This is delightful, and in spite of the reluctance of my companions I am determined if I can to follow this interesting but difficult stream to its source.

It is now a beautiful day, the sun is out with a bright blue sky, and "onwards" is the word with me. Having dined the men, got into my canoe again at 1/4 before

3. Stream shallow and crooked, Peter frequently out hauling the canoe. Very difficult and rough rapids over ledges of conglomerate. At 1/2 past 3 stopped to cut a thick pine which laid across the stream, now reduced to 30 feet wide. At 4 p.m. got into our canoes, looks like water smooth and deep, I suppose we are near the lake. The shore formed of low ledges of greenstone. Beautiful afternoon. Good deal of pine. This land is evidently high, as the water has been rapid and strong for several miles. About 1/4 past four we emerged into a pretty serpentine lake trending to the West, gave three cheers on entering it. Following it up for about 3/4 of a mile we came to another narrow brawling rapid. Here I got out, and accompanied by James, walked through the woods until we came in sight of another lake with some mountains bearing N. 80° W. Sent Wilkinson, who had come up with us, back to order the canoes on. In 1/4 of an hour old Peter, good creature, came paddling along. In a quarter of an hour we reached the beautiful lake of Millinocket, or many islands. It is studded with a great number of islands. The N.W. wind has made the waves high, and in turning round a promontory of greenstone to reach a beach near which to camp, we should have filled but for the skill of Peter. The other canoes also escaped narrowly. Some of the party took some large trout & chub in the first lake. The lofty chain West of us evidently lies at the source of the Millinocket, for there must be another stream coming in at the West end of this lake, itself most likely issuing from another lake, the waters of which are probably furnished by the lofty hills before me. The sun sets brilliantly over those hills at this instant whilst I am writing. The chain of those hills is well-defined, running N.E. & S.W. On my left I also see the continuation of the ridge we have so long followed. A most beautiful evening. The people are preparing our quarters, our servants are cooking some large fish, and I have been collecting some fine specimens of porphyry, greenstone trap with analcime, and various curious minerals of the locality. After a hearty meal laid down to rest.

Friday, September 20th. Rose early as usual and went to the shore of the lake, leaving all sleeping. The lofty hills are now well defined, probably eight miles from us. Another and lower ridge interposes itself between them and us, forming probably the West shore of this lake. The Indian method of forming words after the polysynthetic mode is admirable; from Menich, an island, they form Milnekak, many islands, preserving the first and last sound. Had our breakfast at 7. Mr. Wilkinson took sketches and bearings of the hills, bearing generally N. 7° W., and at 8 m. before 8 a.m. got into my canoe and steered across the lake, leaving my son James to follow with the barometer. Col. Mudge, who has none of the spirit of adventure, preferred remaining behind to fish. A fine ridge on the S. shore of the lake, running from N.N.E. to S.S.W. The shores of this lake are covered with boulders, large and small. Passed a small promontory, the strata running N.E. & S.W., the continuous part of the ridge lying on our left hand...a fine view of the Munsungan mountains.

This is a most beautiful lake, a fine expanse of water, studded with islands covered with cedar, spruce &c, the shores thickly studded with trees, and lofty hills in the distance, covered to the top with trees. A couple of loons complaining. Reached the West shore at 10 m. past 9. I estimate the lake 4 miles long. Here I found the inlet which, after removing the obstructions, I entered, and at 30 m.

past 9 entered by a deep inlet without any rapids another small lake about a mile long, covered with bulrushes for 200 yards, then clear water. At the head of this lake to the right, a ridge. Reached the West shore of this 2nd lake (to name it) at 10 m. past 10 a.m. So the lake is about 1 3/4 miles long. On reaching the inlet heard a fall of water, so we are not at the summit level. This inlet not admitting our canoes, we landed, and accompanied by my son, walked about 1/2 a mile through the woods to another small lake, about 3/4 of a mile long. The hill we saw at our camping place, which bore N. 86 3/4 W. eight miles distant as we computed, bears now N. 76° W. from the East end of this lake. The probability is that other inlets and small lakes would bring us near to the Allagash Lake. But I pursued my course in this direction no further, wishing to find out a portage to the Penobscot and desirous of taking the barometrical height of the dividing ridge near its waters.

At 11 a.m. I set out on my return to the eastward. At 6 m. before 12 m. reached Lake Millinocket, having used my umbrella successfully for a sail. At 8 m. before 12 m. reached the East shore of the lake, being 17 m. less than in going, owing to the umbrella and slight current. Continued down the rapid and found Col. M. wrapt up in his fishing and catching a great many small fish with bait. Dined the men, and at 2 p.m. started in search of a portage to the Penobscot. Col. M. never had the curiosity to ask me where I had been or what I had seen. We now begin to see signs of the moose, both on land and in the shallow water amongst the nelumbium. A great deal of pine about Lake Millinocket, but small trees. At 1/4 past 3 p.m. passed the jam and got into dead water for a while, 3 miles. Pine trees on the stream, a good many. This is the 11th day we are out from the Great Falls, and M. has not yet shaved himself once, nor washed himself for aught I have seen. At 1/2 past 4 p.m. passed the lumberers' camp, and at 5 p.m. joined our men at the mouth of the Munsungan. Opposite the mouth of this stream, ledges of slate altered by greenstone trap run due N.E. & S.W. These are the beds of the Aroostook Falls which we have followed thus far. A remarkable verification of my hypothesis.

Col. M. came in last to the encampment last night, having filled his canoe at the rapids and got everything wet through. A singular piece of gaucherie, everyone else having passed comfortably. I dried the register of our barometrical observations which I delivered to him, and I afterwards found it lying on the ground near the fire where it might have been burnt up, and all our altitudes lost. (*Questo signore non è di verun utilità, e sarebbe stato ben fatto lasciandolo a casa sua*).[40] Pitched our tent at the old place, and the usual ceremonies of cooking &c being performed, supped and lay down.

Saturday, September 21st. Up early, dressed and shaved. Rather cloudy morning. Bustled about and got everyone up *eccuato il signore, ché è sempre ultimo.*[41] Prospect of fine morning. Started up the Munsungan at 35 m. before 8 a.m. Course N. 70° W., a narrow brawling stream 40 feet wide. 5 m. past 8, course W., stream wider, rather shallow but got along well. 30 m. past 8, conglomerate

---

40 This man is of no use whatsoever; it would have been better if he had been left at home.

41 Except the gentleman, because he is always last.

boulders in the bed of the stream. 1/4 before 9, came to a jam and obliged to cross a portage on our left hand. This took us an hour, got wet in a slough, kindled a fire and dried my feet. At 10 m. before 10, got in the canoe again, course S. 80°W. Proceed very slowly on account of the rapids and shallow water, the men being half the time in the water, hauling. James and myself got out on the left bank to lighten the canoe, a horrid thicket and swamp. Peter got ahead of us and made me walk farther than I wished. Came up with the men at 1/2 past 1 p.m. where they were kindling a fire to cook their dinner. The Mooseleuk Mountains in sight about two miles off. Although we have been on the water five hours this morning, I do not think we have made more than eight miles. The Munsungan evidently has a much greater fall than the Millinocket, 2/3rds of which is dead water, yet we estimated its fall at 30 feet.

At 3 p.m., the canoe with the sappers and instruments not having reached us, sent a man on foot to meet them. Thibodeau who poles them is said to have been sick this morning. At 10 m. past 3, started again, deep water. Continued struggling along until 1/4 before 6 p.m. when a ledge crossing the stream and a portage being necessary, I resolved to encamp and halted the party. We soon got our camp settled, and a good blazing fire of cedar, when having heartily supped of trout and biscuit, I turned in. Parsons, on account of a large stump being necessarily left in that part of the tent where I sleep, had arranged my bed so curiously that I hardly knew how to get into it.

Sunday, September 22nd. Rose early after a refreshing night. Had an opportunity of inspecting my four-poster by daylight. First, a large quantity of spruce boughs next to the damp ground, then an oil cloth, next the thin mattress, with my blankets laid N.N.E.-S.S.W. On my right was another oil cloth set up on its edge to keep the two from me on the right side of the tent. On the left was my trunk near my left shoulder, brightened by a box of dried salmon, and further on a large bag used to carry pork over the portages. At the foot, my water proof *sac de nuit* with my clothes, and my rifle near it. On a small box of stones at the right of my feet, my clothes were placed with my dressing case, and on my right my dry shoes on the stump. Next to me, but at right angles to me, laid my son on his spruce boughs and mattress, and at the extreme end of the tent laid Col. Mudge, parallel to James, with all sorts of contrivances his servant had got up for his master, the two servants being extremely jealous of each other's talents in this way, and I believe it was owing to Col. M's servant screening him the night before with a box of hams that I was favoured last night with the box of dried salmon right under my nose. But they certainly make us as comfortable as the nature of the case admits.

This part of the country is very flat near the river, but rises a little back. The timber is spruce and cedar principally, with some small birch. On the ridges back hardwood grows, such as maple, large birch, beech &c. The ground is not very stony and would make a good farming country, especially for meadow. Generally it may be considered a first rate grass country. My old Indian Peter was encamped last night very comfortably. I stumbled upon him in the woods, his birch canoe was inclined on its side, his fire close to him, and he sitting on his blanket eating his supper. Mr. Wilkinson reports the fall of water over the ledge to be between four and five feet, so we must cut a short portage round it. This morning I roused the party. Col. also early, and got everything packed at 1/4 before 7 a.m. At that hour Fahr. 43°. Reached the other end of the portage at 8 a.m., great many moose tracks, rain. At 1/2 past 9, embarked again and turning the first bend had a part of the Mooseleuk in front of us. Course N. 45° W., deep water.

At 10 a.m. reached a small but very pretty lake about a mile and a half long, and about 600 yards wide. A bold ridge on our right running N.E. & S.W., in part at least 1,200 feet high. Due W. the peak is apparently much higher. This ridge, like all the rest, is densely wooded to the very summit, not a crag is to be seen. The ridge is apparently [blank] miles long. But when I have ascended it shall be better able to judge. Having reached a channel, very shortly leading to another lake of about the same size, and the squadron not being arrived from the portage, I stopped to fish with very good luck, taking in half an hour about 16 pounds weight of chub, some weighing 2 lbs, and a fish of the salmon trout species still larger weighing 3 lbs, called by the Indians *Memak*, by the Acadians *Touladi*, and by the Nova Scotians *Tocque*. The canoes being come up at 1/2 past 12, crossed the lake with a prospect of fine weather to ascend the mountain. The lake turns to N. 45° W., had a fine view of Mt. Katahdin bearing due S. Old Peter says it is the Mattawamkeag Mountain, but he is mistaken this time. N.B. He was right.

At 1 p.m. stopped on the East shore of the lake to dine the men. Discovered that we had come away from this morning's portage without our dog Tuksey, the young Indian Michel, a reckless fellow, having neglected to take him into his canoe. I was sorry for it, we had become attached to the dog and he to us, the poor fellow unless he has the wit to make his way on the lake shore will be starved and die.

At 3 p.m. got into the canoe again and proceeded up the lake, course N. 25° W., a fine afternoon, warm and rather cloudy. At 1/2 past 3 p.m. reached the inlet of the lake, a small brawling stream, rather rapid and requiring the use of the pole. Had to stop to cut away some trees; reach another lake at 1/2 past 4 p.m. The lake is about 1 1/2 miles across, with a well defined chain of lofty hills in front, N. 80° W. This is a country of highlands as much as Scotland. This 3rd lake is particularly pleasing, a very high peak to the right bears N. 25° E. [sketch here of lake and mountains.] This appears as high as Mars Hill, and must be visited tomorrow. At 5 p.m. reached the West end of the lake, where the navigation ceases, the inlet being insufficient to float a bateau. Here we encamped. Felt unwell, a return of the old complaint in my head, owing to ever anxiety about the business I am engaged in, the whole conduct of it having devolved upon myself. Upon such occasions, devoting all the powers of my mind to my undertakings, I overtake the nervous system and sometimes suffer correspondingly, being unable from extreme nervousness to dismiss the subject from my mind, night or day. Went to bed early.

Monday, September 23rd. Rain during the whole night, felt very unwell. Rose between six to 7 a.m., felt better. Wind N.W., with prospect of fair weather. Our party up late this morning, and myself not dressed and shaved until 7. The Col. has not shaved yet, to my surprise he called for water to wash this morning. A beard of 13 days! Prepared for an excursion to the mountain, and for cutting out a portage to a small lake which is the last of the Munsungan waters, and where I expect to find our sappers with Mr. Hansard. Mr. Wilkinson reports that from the peak he ascended yesterday afternoon he had a very fine view of the whole country, that to the Southwest, in the direction we are proceeding, he saw nothing but a mass of mountains, but that they cross each other in such a manner that it is difficult to make out the continuous ridge, especially the subordinate ones. But that it is a vast country of highlands. At the summit of the peak the greenstone cuts through the slate, and that the slate ran N.E. & S.W. He brought me a specimen from which I find the slate, like all the others in commination with the traps, is metamorphic.

After breakfast got the people together to ascend the mountain, and at 20 m. past 9 a.m. crossed the lake and began to cut our way, 4 axemen following the compass and the rest of our people with the barometers. Col. Mudge, James and myself following the axemen. Met with a swamp a mile broad. In two hours reached the foot of the mountain, up which we began to ascend. The maples, birches and beeches continued to within 300 feet of the top; here the spruces begin. In the apex of the mountain was nothing but loose rock, a quartzose greenstone with pyrites, such as we met about the 15 Sep. on the Aroostook. Near the top the rock presented a surface with a plume of about 70°. Here Col. Mudge stopped, nor with every offer of assistance could we prevail on him to advance any further. The ascent was steep but not dangerous with care. I imagine he has not a good head for heights. The rest of us reached the summit...where we immediately began to fell the timber to enjoy the magnificent view all round the horizon, being much favoured by the weather which has set in fine with a brisk N.W. wind. From the summit of this hill which is [blank] feet above the sea as measured by our barometers, we have a very extensive view of the truly mountainous country. 30 miles to the South, Mount Katahdin raises his dark bald mass, between that mountain and us a long chain of lofty hills about 1,200 feet high arise; at our feet winds the pretty lake we came up yesterday. South 45° East an extensive chain runs N.E. & S.W. This chain, which when we first saw on our right on the Munsungan Lake, appeared mountainous, now dwindles into the third class of hills. The same may be said of all the ridges not exceeding 600 to 700 feet. From the height I am now writing they appear insignificant, just as this mountain would from Katahdin which is near 5,000 feet high,[42] but those ridges of 400 to 700 feet look very high from the surface of the lakes and in fact are so. In whatever direction we look around the horizon, from this summit, nothing but chains and mountains can be seen. This is as much a Highland country as Scotland, and nothing is more obvious than that an immense barrier of highlands extends from the sources of the Chaudière to the western termination of the Baie des Chaleurs. Our men are cutting down the trees to the S.W. which are very numerous, to give us a view of that quarter. At about 1/2 past 2 p.m. I sent my son with the sappers and the instruments to join the Col. at the foot of the peak, with directions to proceed to the camping place where we would join them before night. The observations and sketches to be made here are too important and I presume it is necessary for me to remain until the last moment. Had a large fire made to show

---

42 Actually 5,268 feet.

our smoke to Mr. Hansard with the supplies, but no symptoms appear of his answering it. The last lake we came up has a narrow pass where it turns to the Northwest. I observe from hence the reason is that it passes through to a continuation of the ridge running S. 45° East; the ridge being hard, the water has not been able to work a broad passage: the ridge to the left of the passage extends far to the S.W. [sketch here.] These lakes then are the bed of the ancient river, which when the waters of the continent subsided, has worked its way through the ridge. Before that subsidence it is probable that the waters of the Allagash and the Munsungan were united. I could see the Allagash waters from the mountains. At 10 m. past 4 p.m., having completed our observations and sketches, left the mountain, and after a severe walk through the swamp and down the mountain's steep sides, reached the lake again in 1h 25m, being less than one half of the time it took us to ascend. Got into the canoe, and having reached the portage, walked it to where the stream is navigable, but to my surprise found the men encamped, taking advantage of my absence, the lazy rascals, as they always do in this Province, sneaked from their work and thus cut our day's work short near 4 miles. The truth is, when they do not see examples of energy and vigilance set by ourselves, they take every liberty they can. On reaching our camp I felt very weak, owing to my indisposition, and for the first time drank a little brandy & water. After making a hearty meal and drying my clothes, laid down to rest.

Tuesday, September 24th. Arose stiff, between 6 and 7 a.m., *l'amico* [Mudge] was not ready for breakfast until 1/2 past 7. In an expedition of this kind there ought to be but one head, to plan and to command; if there are two, and one rises at 6 and is ready, and the other makes him wait until 8, the subordinates themselves are sure to follow the example of the lazy one, misunderstandings take place, the service is not well performed, and what is of the utmost consequence upon this occasion, the precious time is lost, more especially precious at this time when the fine season is drawing to a close, and the days are becoming short. The cold weather will soon overtake us, and for an hour of fine weather we now lose every morning, we shall soon have to pay by so many hours of cold weather and suffering. All this is improper and unjust, both to the public and to myself, and whatever may be the amiable qualities of another, I never will be associated again thus unequally, or indeed at all.

At 1/4 past 9 a.m. commenced the portage of 1 1/2 miles, through which we had to open a road for the canoes and packages. Got into my canoe at the small lake at 1/2 past 11 a.m. This last portage bore from the South and N. 25° W. At noon got to the end of our navigation and were obliged to make another portage of 2 miles S. 80° W. Peter went before to mark the line, and I followed with John Friel to blaze it well. We reached the water 1/4 before 2 p.m., when I sent old Peter further forward to mark another short portage, and stayed myself to make a fire for the men to cook their dinner, sending Friel to hasten the men on to the dining place. This cutting out portage and trampling over logs and through marshes is very fatiguing, but must be done in passing from the headwaters of one stream to those of another. This is what we are now doing. The little lake we are now nigh to is the last of our number, being the headwaters of the Munsungan, and tomorrow I hope to pass into the waters of the Allagash.

Whilst lying by a small fire I had made, believing myself perfectly alone, I heard a rustling noise and turning towards it saw the face of an Indian, with a red cap on his head and a gun in his hand, coming creeping along, prying with his sharp eyes. I jumped up, not knowing him, but he immediately recognized me and came forward with a cheerful face, extending his hand. It was Louis Bernard whom I had sent round with Mr. Hansard to the Allagash. Thus my anxiety was terminated. I learnt from him that all our sappers were arrived in safety at the 4th lake and were now within 12 miles of us. He delivered me a note from Hansard confirming the intelligence. Our people not arriving, I went back and learnt they had not yet left the portage of the morning. There I proceeded in my canoe and found the last things embarking. Mr. Wilkinson, our quartermaster, is a very clever surveyor and in his way a very useful man, but totally incompetent as a head to such an undertaking. He does not know how to command, and lets the men do as they please. Five o'clock being arrived, I am obliged to encamp, and with some difficulty found a situation. Here when we had got our tent pitched, I took occasion to rate Mr. W. and to explain to him that this indolent manner of getting through the country was exceedingly disappointing to me, and that I insisted upon the camp being struck tomorrow morning at 1/2 past 7. Laid down at 1/2 past 8 p.m.

Wednesday, September 25th. Rose at 1/2 past 5 a.m. and got the men up. Had our breakfast at 7. I gave Mr. W. another lecture and explained to him that every hour's loss now would cost us three hours of suffering in cold weather. Col. M. complained of having passed a cold night and expressed his apprehension he should not be able to get through the undertaking. Perceiving that he was in some distress of mind, I engaged my word to him to set him at liberty before the severe season had commenced, engaging to do all the severe work at the close of the season myself. Having comforted him, I explained to Wilkinson my plans and satisfied him that on his own account and that of the men he must make greater exertions. By 1/2 past 7 a.m. I had the party afloat, and having reached the portage, we cleared it and passed it by 9 a.m.

I now despatched the axemen ahead to clear a short portage at the end of the stream of 30 rods, 1/4 mile, N. 50° E., and at 10 a.m. followed them to a small lake, being the headwater of the Munsungan. Reached it at 1/2 past 10 a.m. This lake is a beautiful sheet of water, nearly oblong, about 3/4 mile long, S. 80° W., and 500 yards wide. The hills which surround it have pretty summits, well clothed with hardwood, and a few spruce. They are about 200 ft. high. A beautiful morning, bright and fresh, N.W. wind. Reached the West end of the pretty lake at 1/2 past 12 m. The Indian Bernard, not being returned to report the direction in which our portage is to be made, I let the men dine to save time, and went out to take a sketch whilst James fished. At the East end of the lake we have a fine view of the mountain, the one ascended the day before yesterday. Saw the gap we had made by cutting the trees down. It bears East from the point where I am. [sketch here.] From this place I see that mountain is only one peak of a chain extending N.E. & S.W. Found that Wilkinson had not put us pork up for the men. Sent a Canadian for some, the fellow did not return until 1/4 past 3. Entered the portage, N. 20° W. Found the hands hard at work, with some apprehension we should not get to water tonight.

About 4 p.m. had the great satisfaction of meeting Hansard who had come on to meet us. He conveyed to us the pleasing intelligence of having killed two moose, so our camp will be well supplied with food, and the men's spirits kept up. Met Nadeau and the Indians who say we are about 2 miles from the first lake. As it would be impossible for us to reach it tonight on account of our tent, beds and provisions being left behind, I directed Nadeau and Bernard with some hands to clear to a brook half a mile ahead and to kindle a fire for tonight's camp, whilst I sent the rest of the hands to bring up the baggage, returning also myself to look up Col. Mudge whom I found half a mile back lagging along. I begin now to wish him in Quebec, being afraid he will break down in the woods, which would be a great encumbrance to me, as the worst job in the world is to get a knocked up man through a wilderness. This portage according to appearance will be full 3 miles. Went back to cheer the men up and encourage them on. The intelligence of the moose meat seems to have produced a great effect, so close is the connection between a man's temper and his belly. At about 1/2 past 5 p.m. got them all up and a good fire started. Supped and laid down.

Thursday, September 26th. A rainy night. My travelling shoes left out all night in the rain, had some trouble getting them dry. A little past 7 a.m. got our breakfast and made preparations to start again. Mr. Hansard thinks that in one hour we shall reach the first Allagash lake; this is about 2 miles long (1 mile N. 70° W.), then comes a portage of 3/4 of a mile, then a sort of lagoon 1/4 of a mile to a large lake across which the course was N. 70° W. to a portage. The rain poured down in torrents all this morning. We crossed this lake 3 miles, part of the way in a somewhat high sea, in a canoe with the Canadians, James and myself, the rain pouring all the way, and wet and cold. On reaching the portage, we with some difficulty kindled a fire and got dry. At this small lake James and myself visited a recent beaver dam built this summer; it extended across a small brook about 40 feet and was three feet high. This Louis Bernard says was to make a winter residence and was built by one pair this summer. Portage was about half a mile. Col. Mudge killed three partridges on the road, and one of the men killed a fourth with a stone. The portage N. 60° W. We now came to a small and very shallow lake full of lotus and nelumbium, 1/2 a mile long N. 50° W. Thence my son James and myself made another march across a portage of about one mile, N. 50° W., and at 1/4 past 4 p.m. reached the East shore of the 4th lake [Wallagasquigwam or Churchill Lake].

Across the island in a direction N. 50° W. we saw the smoke of Hansard's encampment, who with a total want of judgement has made the depot on the other side of the lake. A strong N.W. wind has made an angry sea upon which we cannot trust ourselves and canoes. We are therefore cut off from our supplies which we have made such efforts to reach, and if the storm continues three days, which it may well do, this being the equinox, we are without food for our party and for the still more numerous party behind us who are almost out of provisions. Such an inconsiderate step in a man of 50 years old and who has been an officer in the army is without excuse, and I have rated this weak talkative man. In consequence of this folly, we have been obliged to put up our tent hastily in the dark, and making a hasty and bad meal, to lie down and forget the vexation in sleep, first despatching Hansard across the lake with two men in a birch canoe to bring provisions for Wilkinson's party in the rear early in the morning.

Friday, September 27th. After an uneasy night, and getting to sleep towards morning, Hansard having returned with provisions awoke me. Dressed, washed and crossed the lake in a birch canoe with my son, Col. M. and Hansard in another, leaving the servants and baggage to come afterwards. On reaching Hansard's depot and looking towards the lake, we heard cries of distress, one of our canoes being evidently upset and no men in it. I instantly despatched three canoes to the spot, about a mile off. A second canoe remained at the place. With our telescopes we now could see the two sappers, McQueen and Hearnden, but not my servant Parsons and Thomas, the servant of Col. M. We felt a conviction now that they were drowned, and taking it for granted my letter case with all my documents and vouchers, as well as my baggage, were lost, I felt as if a great misfortune had befallen me. Parsons had conducted himself with such propriety, had shown such zeal to make me comfortable, and was such a clever and respectable man that I was in great anguish of mind. At length the relief we sent reached the spot, and on the party making back again for the depot I had the very great satisfaction of seeing Parsons & Thomas in a canoe. On landing they were so cold and pale they could not speak. McQueen relates that his canoe was a little behind the one in which Parsons & Thomas were, without anyone to conduct them. Undertaking to paddle themselves across and the waves rough, and sitting on the cross bars instead of the bottom, they by their awkwardness upset the canoe. Parsons could swim, but Thomas was nearly drowned, when McQueen seized him by the collar and saved him. Fortunately there was nothing in the canoe but a fishing rod and umbrella belonging to Col. M. which were lost. My mind being thus relieved, I went to breakfast, when a new alarm was raised for Michael Curran, an Irishman who had been particularly attentive to us, and most useful in everything connected with our personal comfort. He was missing and I immediately despatched a couple of canoes to look for him.

In the meantime I had the tent pitched, the floor neatly strewed with spruce, examined the clever log house Hansard had made for our provisions, and brought up my journal. He certainly has pitched his camp in a pleasant place, fronting S. 50° E., with a fine range of mountains of which we had a view from the crooked lake of Munsungan. In fact it is a very agreeable place and here I must remain two or three days for Wilkinson.

Nothing is more surprising than the indifference and listlessness of Col. M. He takes no interest in anything but his meals, makes no observations, and is so totally mindless and passive that he would not only be utterly incapable of finding his way back, but would let me carry him to China without concerning himself about any occurrence foreign to his own wants. Never was a greater mistake made by man than he has committed, in leaving his own happy home to come on an expedition where he is of no use, and from which he longs to be delivered, having some fearful apprehension on his mind that he is in danger of perishing by the cold weather, as it would seem to me, for I cannot understand a man's acting so passive a part as he does. I have just told him he must make some observations for longitude here, now that we have leisure, but he will not do it. Neither have we had the variation once ascertained, so that my general map is in danger of being regulated by approximation. If he took the least interest in our exploration, or could be relied upon at all, we could separate here; he could go to the South to examine the N.E. range, whilst I attended to the re-organization of the party, and our route to the S.W. But having everything to attend to, I am obliged to stay and await the arrival of Wilkinson's party. In the meantime the barometrical register is yet in pencil marks, and is besides in danger of being lost every day. I never will come under any responsibility of this kind to government again unless I am permitted to choose assistants known to me to possess the requisite qualities. If any accident were to happen to me, all our labour hitherto would be lost, as Col. M. could bring no results out of it. What aggravates his conduct is that he has not shaved since we left the Great Falls on the 9th, now 19 days, and that he is so inattentive to propriety as always to sit at our meals with his hat on, a perfect specimen of uncleanliness. He thinks of nothing and talks of nothing but eating and smoking, and drinking his brandy & water.

Having got our tent clean and the floor strewed with fresh green boughs, I got out my letter case and wrote to Sir John Harvey, then took a walk on a very pretty beach we have, collected some minerals, and at 6 dined of excellent fish, boiled and fried, fried moose meat, and broiled spruce partridges, with London porter for the first time. A magnificent repast for the woods. At 7 p.m. went to my bed.

Saturday, September 28th. Rain in the night; on rising at 7 a.m. a cloudy cool morning, Fahr. at 30°, a few flakes of snow; about 8 began to clear up with a West wind. Old Louis Bernard indisposed, gave him a little brandy and some medicine. He overworked himself the other day. After breakfast Mr. Hansard and the young Indian Michel went across an extensive bay to the South to endeavour to trace the moose cow wounded the other day. I was somewhat tempted to go with them, desirous of seeing one of them alive, but having taken medicine with much writing to do, I gave up the idea. About an hour afterwards a gun was heard in their direction, and upon reconnoitering with a glass their canoe was seen bottom upwards. Old Peter the Indian immediately went off in his birch to see if any accident had happened, and on nearing the place he found they had upset in the lake but had righted their boat. In half an hour Hansard arrived and related that being on their return across the bay, three ducks flew over their heads, when upon firing at them the gun recoiled, knocked him over on the side of the canoe and rolled him into the water. This upset it and threw the Indian also overboard. Hansard now swam for the shore about 150 yards, but hearing the Indian cry out for relief, who did not know how to swim, he very properly turned back to assist him. The poor fellow clung to the boat; after many treads during which the canoe rolled over frequently, Hansard got on the bottom of the canoe and recovered the paddle, directing the Indian to sink himself low in the water and hold on by the back of the canoe. He succeeded happily in paddling them ashore. They were about 1/2 an hour in the water, and on their arrival were pale and shivering from exhaustion and evaporation of natural heat, but a fire, dry clothes, and a little brandy brought them to again. This second accident was owing also to want of judgement. The gun had been two days loaded with ball, and Hansard had put an additional load of duck shot in it. The slightest irregular movement in a canoe will endanger it, and a gun thus fired into the zenith was very likely to produce these consequences. I hope it will be a lesson to them all.

After a windy day, the evening cleared up bright. We made our evening repast, the men went out to spear touladi by torchlight, and between eight and nine I laid down to rest. This day I wrote letters to Mr. Fox, Mr. Backhouse,[43] and Sir John Harvey, intending to send them by the men I propose discharging when Wilkinson arrives.

Sunday, September 29th. Cold frosty night, Fahr. 28° at 7 a.m.; a beautiful sky, a little cloudy and N.W. wind. Rose the first in the camp, washed, dressed and shaved, put a coat on and announced my intention of leading the service, as some evidence we had not quite relapsed into barbarism. After breakfast read divine service, our servants and two or three of the people attending. In the course of the day Mr. Wilkinson and his party arrived, when immediately took measures to re-organize the party and discharge all but 15 hands, distributing the provisions in such a manner as to give those discharged sufficient to carry them home, and reserving what is necessary for ourselves. I omitted to note that on Saturday eight Penobscot Indians on a hunting excursion for beaver &c stopped at our camp. They spoke English pretty well and were all of mixed blood. They resided at Old Town in Maine, and were going to trap down the Allagash. They also had killed a moose. We obtained some information from them of the best mode of getting into the S. sources of the Saint John. This day was cloudy and we could not obtain an observation for latitude, neither have we got the variation yet. This is a constant subject of fruitless regret to me, but where there is no zeal there is no system to be expected. Wrote several hours today, and after dinner retired early to bed.

Monday, September 30th. Rose a little before 6 a.m., Fahr 27°, a fine but rather cloudy morning. Everyone lazy, can get nothing done. After breakfast began to make arrangements for re-organizing the party; divided into 3 bodies. One, consisting of 22 persons discharged, belonging to Madawaska, the Great Falls and Fredericton. This party goes under the guidance of Morrison, a clever man from Fredericton. He will also take in charge some superfluous provisions remaining behind after allotting for our future wants. The other party goes with me. I have determined to go further south, and cut through the woods to Woolastaquagam [Baker Lake], a lake on the S.E. branch of the Saint John, taking three birch canoes and two logs, and sufficient provisions to last us ten days. My party will consist of myself, my son, Mr. Wilkinson, my servant, McQueen the sapper, Peter the Indian, and six working men with two tents & the instruments. The 3rd party will be managed by Hansard and will go down the Allagash to its mouth, then up the Saint John to its S.W. source to meet me at Woolastaquagam with the provisions. Col. Mudge on account of the safe and continuous navigation prefers to go with this party. These arrangements, the making out the accounts of the discharged men, and repairing our boats and canoes will detain us all day here. Col. M. got an observation at 12, being a fine day. I hope he got an azimuth

---

43 John Backhouse (c.1783-1845), permanent undersecretary, Foreign Office.

for variation. Dined at 1/2 past 6 p.m., and at 1/2 past 8 laid down; a rainy night.

Tuesday, October 1st. A cloudy but dry morning. This was a morning of perplexing occupation to me, having to arrange the departure of the three parties, subdivide the provisions, pay the men in drafts on the bank. Wilkinson is quite incompetent to such business, and Col. M never offered me the least assistance. At length about 20 m. past 11 a.m., took leave of Mudge and Hansard, got into my canoe and started down the lake.

Course N. 60° West, 1/2 a mile across the lake to a narrow sedgy passage about 80 feet wide until 10 m. past 12 m. Course S. 70° W., then a small round lake 1 m. across, S. 70° W. to another reedy passage of 100 ft. S.70° W., with an eminence 200 feet high in front across Lake Pagaquaymuk which reached at 1/2 before 1 p.m. This lake extends 1 1/2 miles to the N. on our right, and in 3/4 m. from its entrance bends to a course of S. 20° W. for 6 or 8 miles, about 1 mile wide. Wind S.W. and high, finding no safe place to place our canoes whilst the men were dining. Crossed the lake 1 mile to get under the lee of some hills, the waves being rather high. Saw a large bear on the shore. On landing, Peter and the others went after the bear which got off. This is a very beautiful and long lake of about 10 m. as Peter says; fine sloping hills come down to it, the whole aspect being very pleasing. 1 1/4 p.m., landed to dine the men. Got some beautiful specimens of greenstone trap.... At 20 m. to 3 got into our canoes again, fair weather, calm water. Course due S. At 16 m. before 4 p.m., course S. 20° E. Katahdin bearing S. 45° E., high. Being about 20 m. past 4, crossed to a fine island, smooth water, course S. 12° E., Katahdin bearing S. 15° E., covered with snow. 1/2 past 4 p.m., S. 70° W., a ridge before us, 3 m. off, running N.E. & S.W. At 1/2 past 5 p.m. got to the end of the lake Pagaquaymuk and found the inlet coming in with a brawling noise, there being as it would appear a fall between the next lake South of this and us.

Camped on the east side in a nice clear place and had the light round tent put up. We are comparatively comfortable, having got rid of the crew of blackguards I discharged yesterday, and free to dispose of the time, the habits of my companion M. retarding the service very much at times. Supped of moose meat and potatoes and laid down to rest at 8 p.m.

Wednesday, October 2nd. Rose before 6 a.m. and had the beds packed and everything got ready for starting before breakfast. At 7 a.m. embarked and went up the inlet, a shallow stream about 60 feet wide and rather rapid. In 40 m. reached Lake Umgenaygamuc [Chamberlain Lake], our course having been about S. 70° W., 3/4 mile. Crossed the lake, course S., to a point on the S. shore with a pretty beach where we had our breakfast cooked. This Lake Umgenaygamuc is an extensive sheet of water about 15 miles long. We crossed it from N. to S., but its length is from N.W. to S.E., with a great bay extending from near the foot of the lake to the N.E. In crossing the lake we had a perfect view of Mount Katahdin, saw its shape: there is a fine set of mountains between us and it, apparently extending a long way to the N.E. & S.W. This is I suppose a continuation of the Bald Mountains. Rock here a fine light coloured greenstone trap, quite prismatic. A singular white bright spot appears on the side of the ridge between us and

Katahdin, bearing S. 20° E. from the point where we breakfasted. Peter says he has always seen it, even by moonlight. It appears to be a mass of quartz reflecting the light. At 1/4 before 10 a.m. got into my canoe again, sunny morning, wind S.W., rather mild. Had a view of the N.E. ridge between us and Katahdin, running about 30 miles. At 35 m. past 11 a.m. came to the inlet, having steered S. to it. It is a very small bay on the right hand. Here we had to walk a few rods on account of the shallow rapid, then got into the canoe in still water.

John Friel, like an ass, lost himself, and we remained more than an hour firing guns and halloing to him. Sent a man into the woods after him and recovered him. He heard our sounds but could not on account of the wind and the trees distinguish the quarter they came from. Before we reached a small lake called Paquaygomus or Mud Lake, we had to traverse an old portage of 1/2 mile S. 40x W. Here we stopped to dine the men on the edge of the lake. My son took a very fine trout. At 1/4 past 3 p.m. got into my canoe again and crossed the Lake Paquaygomus, a round lake about 1 mile across, almost covered with the leaves of the lotus. It well deserves its name of Mud Lake. We arrived at a portage of 1 3/4 miles leading to Lake Obscuskus [Umbazooksus] or Reed Lake. This portage for the first third part is a deep black mire which it would be almost impossible to get through but for the old logs blown down, and other small ones which have occasionally been thrown in, upon which there is some footing to be had. It is a very old portage, wide enough to carry a bateau. The rest of the way is tolerably good, and one part consists of a handsome dry ridge of excellent land. My son and myself crossed the portage first. The lake to the left is very much choked with the lily, but to the right is a pretty open sheet of water about 1 1/2 miles long. Selected a very excellent camping place about 100 yards from the lake, a grove of maples and beeches, and very fertile land.

Generally speaking, the land is very good in this part of the country, capable of maintaining a numerous agricultural population. In beauty nothing can exceed parts of it: extensive lakes with mountains of a lofty kind in the foreground, as on Lake Umgenaygamuc, whilst the hills bordering upon the lake frequently slope down in a very graceful manner. Take the country altogether, it is the most elegant solitude imaginable. About 1/2 past 5 p.m. our men came up with their loads, very much fatigued. Had our tents pitched, fires made, and having supped laid down to rest, the rain pouring down.

Thursday, October 3rd. Heavy rain all night, very often awaking me by dropping through the tent on my face. Arose at 1/4 past 6 a.m., had the fires refreshed, and despatched the men to the other end of the portage for the canoes &c. At 1/2 past 7 a.m. the rain began to abate, directed my son to get the barometers out and suspend them to acquire a settled temperature. We are now at an interesting point, on the axis which divides the waters of the Penobscot from those of the Allagash. The lake now near us, Obscuskus, empties out into the Penobscot and is an Atlantic Ocean water. There is a fine spring near the edge of the lake. Fahr. 47° this morning, and except the maples and a few shrubs which have begun to change, the leaves on the trees are quite fresh, which makes me think we shall have a protracted autumn. After breakfast, took my son with the barometers to the central and dry part of the portage, 3/4 mile from our camp to the N.E., and took the elevation of this particular axis which divides the waters of the Penobscot from those of the Allagash.

It took to past noon before the men had crossed all the things and boats over the portage. At 1/4 past 12 m., made Peter take James & myself to the outlet of the lake which Peter told me was called in his Morriseet tongue Obscusquagam or Reed Lake, and in the Penobscot dialect Obscususkahgumuc. The lake is about 3 miles long. The outlet is at the S.W. end, the lake running N. 20° W. Some mountains are seen in the direction of the head of the lake about N. 50° W., about 20 miles distant, and are probably near the Saint John. At 1/2 past 2 p.m. proceeded down the Obscuskus, a tortuous and very serpentine stream, generally about 20 feet broad and proceeding about S. 20° W. The banks overhang the stream with alders in places, and the sand and mud banks have high grass growing upon them whence the stream takes its name of Obscuskus (long grass).

In this brook we met with a remarkable beautiful trout in great numbers; they came close to the canoes, so that we could discern all their motions, took the bait (pork) into their mouths as if to taste it, but very rarely swallowed it; we however took a few with the hook. Nadeau, one of my men, took a great many with the spear; upon one occasion he brought out two at the end of his spear. They were much attracted by any shining thing and darted at the buoys. We passed nearly an hour observing and taking them, providing ourselves with about 24 lbs weight. The jaws of this trout are very wide, the head, back and tail a dark brown, almost black; large yellow blotches on the sides, and nearer the belly the blotches had bright red spots in them. The belly was of a very bright blood orange colour. The two pectoral, two vertical and the lower fins near the tail were red nearest the body, then dark brown, and edged all with a beautiful white like ivory. The wide jaws were also white. A more beautiful fish I never saw.[44] At 1/2 past 4 p.m., finding a place in this extensive swamp where we could make a decent camp, I stopped for the night, got everything comfortably arranged, and after supper laid down to rest at 1/2 past 7 p.m.

Friday, October 4th. Awoke in the night by a high wind and inferred, it being N.W., we should have fair weather. Arose before six and as soon as possible took James & McQueen with the instruments and Wilkinson to climb, and left camp for a ridge about a mile and a half off. Cut our way through a nasty swamp of a mile, and rose a beautiful ridge about S. 30° W. and N. 30° E. Mr. W. got into a tall spruce but it was so windy he could not make any observations, it being hardly safe to stay in the top of the tree. Saw ridges S.W. from him about 10 miles off. Took barometrical observations and reached camp about 3/4 past 8 a.m. to breakfast. Fahr. 38°. At 1/4 past 10 a.m. loaded the canoes ready for our departure, a fine bright morning. Started at 1/4 past 10 down the Obscuskus, an exceedingly crooked stream of which the general direction is S. 30° W. The ridge continues parallel with our course, but rather depressed. Very cold day, heavy cold clouds; looks as if it were going to snow.

A little past 12 m. came to the mouth of the Kaskumgomac. Near this place

---

44 Probably a description of the brook trout (Salvelinus Fontinalis), a species of char, which is very brightly coloured in October during the spawning season. See Mudge's journal for the same day where, by coincidence, he describes a similar fish.

and on the channel to Chesuncook Lake, two Penobscot Indians had made their camp, drying moose meat and muskrat skins. They had killed a large bull moose with ten tines; I purchased his antlers. His skin measured 8 feet by 6 feet 4 in.; his antlers from tip to tip 5 feet, and the horn 3 ft. 4 in. Took the canoe down to look at Chesuncook Lake, a fine narrow sheet of water, with a view of a mountain bearing S. 15° E. A stormy sea on the Chesuncook, not safe for canoes. Returned to our men at the Indian camp and gave directions for them to cook for dinner. At 20 m. past 2 p.m. got into our canoes and proceeded up the Keeaquagummustic, a very pretty stream. Still water for 1 1/2 miles when a fall about 8 feet occurs over a dyke of greenstone, stratified vertically and quite red as though it had burnt or very much affected by manganese. It took us half an hour to get our canoes over this fall; two miles further which we paddled in 40 minutes we came to a second fall, over another dyke of the same kind, of 7 feet, over which we got our canoes in a 1/4 of an hour. It now became very cold and the N.W. wind high with a wintry appearance in the sky. We paddled along through a broad stream, generally of deep water, and about 150 feet wide, until we reached a very pretty small lake, very angry with the high wind. We coasted the foot of it to the Northeast corner, the waves being sufficiently high to make me anxious about the log canoes, but we all arrived happily at our camping place about 20 m. after 5 p.m. Our course up this stream this afternoon was crooked but the mean was about N. 25° W. We had excellent fires and a good supper. James amused himself with setting fire to the ragged birches which gave a brilliant light. We had abundance of dry wood at this place, and plenty of nice spruce boughs to strew the floor of our tent. Centigrade Ther. 2° at 8 p.m. Laid down at 1/2 past 8.

Saturday, October 5th. A pleasant calm morning and clear sky. Rose the first in the camp and mended our fire. This little lake is about 1 1/2 miles long and nearly as broad, bearing N. 25° W. to the inlet. Made this in 30 m., being 1 1/2 m. The rocks at the N.W. ran exactly N.E. & S.W., a stratified altered slate. Got into the inlet, a fine broad stream 50 feet wide, still water, a quarter of eight a.m. came to shoal water and current. At 1/2 past 8 landed to breakfast on the N. side. Very cold morning and all glad to warm ourselves at the fire. Put worsted stockings on for the first time. Came about 5 miles from the camp; a flat country on each side with great abundance of white birch. This will make a good dairy country. After a comfortable breakfast pursued our course N. 25° W. at 5 m. past 10 a.m. At 15 m. came to shoal and swift water for 150 yards. Rocks quartzose, stratified N.E.& S.W. At 11 a.m. entered a long and difficult rapid. Got out to walk and lighten the canoes. At 20 m. past 12 m. went down to the stream to look at some rocks and came to a ridge of calcareous slate, identical to that of the mouth of Aroostook, well defined as to stratification and dipping N. 35° W. about 50°. This ridge crosses the river due N.E. & S.W. and makes a fall of about 7 feet. This slate has rather singular veins of coarse granular matter in it. Took specimens of these rocks. A hundred yards higher up, directed the men to stop to dine.

At 2 p.m. continued our course, the canoes forcing themselves up the rapids, whilst myself, my son, and the servants walked by a short blazed path which the Indians have used when on hunting parties to pass, with their toboggans or light birch skiffs on their backs, from the lake to deep water below the rapids. At 1/2 past 2 p.m. came to Lake Kiaquagam [Caucomgomoc Lake], a most beautiful sheet of water extending about 5 miles to N. 45° W. and about 2 miles width in places. The extreme beauty of this sheet of water struck everybody. To the South and S.W. a beautiful and lofty ridge of land ran as far as the eye could reach from S.W. to N.E. and continued far beyond the lake. This I take to be the continuation of the highlands from the sources of the Chaudière, a fact which I propose to ascertain after reach Lake Woolastaquagam [Baker Lake]. To the South a very lofty mountain runs near Moosehead Lake, and Katahdin in great majesty with his peak white with snow is full in view, bearing S. 45° E. I never saw a more engaging view presented from any lake in N. America. Towards the head of the lake numerous picturesque islands appear, with a base of slate which on the borders of this lake are green, red and blue, and seem to identify themselves with the Cambrian of the worthy Professor Sedgwick, of whom I always think with great kindness. Went to the head of the lake to see where the inlet was, and then encamped in a dry convenient place. Got our tent up as usual, and after a plentiful supper laid down to rest on clean boughs.

Sunday, October 6th. Arose before daybreak, the first up in the tent as usual, and mended our fire. The owls and the loons made a great noise last night in the woods, and on the lake. Beautiful clear morning, fine sunrise. Took barometrical observations. Got into our canoes a few minutes before 7 a.m. and entered the inlet which is very small and full of obstructions. We had to lift all the things and canoes over two jams, and the men had to haul them in the shallow water the greatest part of the way. Had to walk myself in a villainous alder swamp, out of which I was glad to be relieved, my son James who had got into deep water, returning to look for me. Reached a small lake almost grown up with lotus, being the head water of the [Caucomgomuc]. A small sulphur spring at its East shore, and a fine spring of fresh water near it. The ice on the shallow part of this lake 3/8 of an inch thick. Fahr. 22 at 6 a.m. Here landed to breakfast. We have now a long portage to cut of about seven miles to [Baker Lake]. A beautiful day. Sent Wilkinson on up a tree after breakfast to ascertain what heights are in the direction of the portage, and he reported a very considerable one, being a lofty peak of the chain we saw to the West from Lake Caucomgomuc. Took three axemen, and sending W. before with the compass, crossed the little lake with James, McQueen and the instruments. Nowithstanding our utmost diligence, cutting through perverse swamps &c, we only reached the foot of the peak 20 m. before 5 p.m., when not venturing to trust to the portage at night, especially in dark and difficult swamps, we returned and reached a camp the men had formed from our starting place W. of the little lake. Here we supped and went to rest.

Monday, October 7th. A fine morning, Fahr. 27°. All hands busy packing up for carrying and opening the portage for the canoes. Sent axemen forward, and at 10 m. past 8 a.m. followed them with provisions for breakfast, leaving the rest of our stores ready packed for carrying under a birch canoe to secure them from rain. Stopped at the first brook and made fires for cooking. This brook runs into the small lake we have left, and is of course a Penobscot stream.

After breakfast left men to bring on the loads and open the portage, and proceeded with James, Wilkinson, Nadeau and McQueen, with the instruments, to ascend the mountain, a very arduous task which took us full two hours from its base. It turned out to be, what I had always believed it to be, Campbell's chain from the sources of Chaudière. When on the highest peak, notwithstanding the cloudiness of the morning with a little rain, we saw no ridge to the North or North-west, but the chain of which this peak is a part extends indefinitely to the S.W. to the sources of the Chaudière and to the N.E., an innumerable sequence of ridges and hills, whilst to the S. and S. east other long ridges strike thro' the country N.E. & S.W., with Katahdin in the rear of them, just as that mountain has always appeared to us. The truth is that this whole country is divided by a broad range of highlands running from the Bald Mountains to Mars Hill, of which Campbell's chain[45] follows the N.W. side. This range rises steadily N.E. & S.W. and is sometimes, but rarely, divided into detached masses, the waters of the Penobscot occasionally flowing through the valleys interposed between them from the N.W. side of the range. On the N.W. side of the peak we saw [Baker Lake] and a stream running into it, the head of which appears to be only two miles from our portage. The series of views from this peak [is] most interesting, and particularly important, as they confirm our case.

On the top of the peak we found nothing but stunted spruce trees, the ledges of slate running N.E. & S.W. Remained on the top of the peak until about 4 p.m. [Baker Lake] bears N. 57° W. from this peak to a point, bare-looking like sand on the W. side of the lake, at the entrance to a bay setting off to the W. This ridge of the peak is so narrow (20 yards) that the most extensive view can be seen on each side to the North & South; [Baker Lake] with the whole territory along the Saint John passes through, including Temiscouata as well as Caucomgomuc Lake and the territory of the Penobscot with Katahdin. Came down the mountain very tired, supped and went to bed.

Tuesday, October 8th. Arose a little before 6 a.m., the first in the camp as usual. Rather stiff from the exertions of yesterday. Sent the hands to yesterday's camping place for the rest of the luggage and the boats. A fine morning, Centigrade 12 1/2°, which is about 54 1/2° Fahr. After breakfast Wilkinson went with old Peter to blaze out a continuation of the portage.... The opening of the portage is far to the N.W. and the carrying the boats and provisions both from our old encampment and in advance of our journey, determined me to keep our present camp for the night. James and myself therefore remained stationary. Late at night Wilkinson & Peter returned with information that the N.E. ridge was inaccessible for a portage, it being too lofty to get the boats over. They had climbed it and descended it, slope N.E. as the strata run, and had at length found a crevice which they think accessible. They are of opinion it will only be two miles to manageable water from there and state that they went as far as some springs which are at the sources of the Saint John. At 1/2 past 6 p.m. supped, and laid down at 7 p.m.

---

45 A ridge of highlands surveyed by Colin Campbell, a British surveyor , in 1819.

Wednesday, October 9th. Fine morning, up at 6 a.m., roused the lazy fellows, who are never to get up in the morning. Sent Wilkinson and Peter ahead to blaze out the portage to the crevice. Centigrade 12 1/2° at 7, a fine soft morning. Breakfasted and left the camp at 8 a.m., having sent the men off with some loads, and the axemen to precede them. In half an hour found a dead partridge suspended on a stick, which I suppose has been shot by Peter, having heard the report of a gun, 3/4 of an hour before. Saw a black fly just now, being the first I have seen for several days. At 10 a.m. came to the central and lowest part of the crevice, the South side of which came upon a lair of the moose, their fresh dung lying about in various directions. About 8 appear to have laid there last night. Took barometrical observations at the centre of the crevice. These depressions between the peaks are so low that at a distance the peaks appear to be isolated mounts, but they are all connected by strong ledges of slate run N.E. & S.W. by compass, and I take the direction to show the continuity of this range of highlands.

At 1/2 past 11 a.m. came to another lateral spur of the ridge of considerable height. Had a fine view from the top to the eastward of the whole country, for a great breadth, being filled with highlands. I again saw the confirmation of what I have repeatedly witnessed that from about [Latitude] 46° 30' to about 47° 20', the whole country is occupied by a range of highlands running from N.E. to S.W. by compass, with the strata interrupted in part by the wearing away by diluvial action and by weather, but being in all essential particulars an existing range of highlands. At the particular spur where I now write the whole rocks consist of ledges of schistose blue slate running N.E. & S.W.

Walked on to see whether Wilkinson & Peter had succeeded in finding still water, came to running water of Saint John, sent my son back to hasten on the men with the luggage and provisions. Came up with W. further to the West who had sent Peter to explore nearer to the lake. Returned with W. to the first running water, excessively fatigued walking all day in thickets and swamps, and sat down alone in the swamp with no amusement but my notebook, 4 p.m. About 1/2 past 4 Peter came up and reported that he had followed the swamp two miles further, that it grew more intricate and difficult to move in, without any symptoms of dead water. He had been close to three moose and had chased them a short distance, did not see them, the swamp being too thick; a bull, a cow and her calf, the bull roared very hard. Selected a place to encamp in the swamp, and began to clear it. Sent W. to hasten the men on, and about night they brought in the tents, beds and provisions. Got our fires made as quick as we could, supped and laid down very much fatigued. McQueen saw a cow moose this evening but did not get a shot at her.

Thursday, October 10th. Rainy morning, Fahr. 50°, took barometrical observations. Sent the men to bring up a canoe and some packages left on yesterday's portage. At 1/4 past 9 a.m., having breakfasted, Wilkinson and Peter began to blaze a new line at an angle of 45° to that of yesterday to gain the hardwood land and then change to the stream. We suppose ourselves about 5 miles from Lake Woolastaquagam [Baker Lake], 3 miles which we hope will be still water. Our progress yesterday we estimate at 2 1/2 miles. Had my tents struck about 2 p.m., found the 1st mile through a bad entangled swamp, the rest of the way 1 1/2 on hardwood land, great part of which is very good, with fine slope. We crossed no water during the day, and after sending scouts in advance, and on our right and left, finding no water was to be obtained and the evening coming on, I selected a camp and had our fire built. Here, having collected the party, they made their supper without their usual cup of tea, as we did ourselves, dining on a cold partridge, fried pork and a little London porter.

Some of the birches here were exceedingly ragged, with their bark hanging about them like huge quantities of drapery. We set fire to some of them, and the noise it produced by the sudden combustion almost from bottom to top resembled, as the men at a distance who heard it said, the thundering of a herd of cattle. Some of the trees being rotten at the top took fire there and continued blazing after dark. If Mudge and his party are on the lake and look this way they must observe it. They would upon occasion serve as a good signal from the woods. I observe also when a fire is built at the foot of a lofty tree, the smoke is drawn up the trunk and issues in a column from the top, which would be an excellent signal. Great part of this afternoon we followed an Indian blaze of 3 or 4 years old.

Between 4 & 5 p.m. W. & Peter arrive and report that they have found the navigable stream about 2 1/2 miles from our camp, that the rivulet we encamped upon yesterday is a very insignificant stream which falls into the main S.E. branch of the Saint John above [Baker Lake]. The main branch is navigable he says, for canoes from ten to 15 miles above the head of the lake, and that it trends to the S.W. & W. The sketch I have from an American survey as respects the position of this lake is entirely wrong and has misled us a good deal, altho' it has been occasionally useful.

Friday, October 11th. Fahr. 29°, 7 a.m. This is a beautiful clear sunny morning, and I hope Col. Mudge will have taken advantage of it on [Baker Lake] to take an altitude and azimuth both for latitude and variation. I am ashamed of our proceedings in this particular; we have neither latitude or longitude at any one point, nor has he yet given me the variation, so that I have nothing to govern the adjustment of my topographical observations. This must not be endured any more, and if his indolence or incapacity are to continue this state of things, I have nothing left but to waive all delicacy towards him and have these essentials supplied by my son and myself. I see clearly that I shall never be able to recommend with proper intelligence any future line of demarcation by way of compromise, without having my points fixed by astronomical observation. If this brings about a rupture betwen Col. Mudge and myself, it will not be my fault. I am determined to do my duty. He has not been of the least use to me hitherto, and can do nothing more prejudicial to the enterprise than he has already done, having been totally useless. Without my son I should never have got the barometrical observations, and it is most fortunate he consented to come. What is most surprising is that the Col. must see that all the men see his unfitness and indolence and yet makes no exertions. His conduct is to me incomprehensible. Wilkinson says the variation has increased to the westwards at the rate of 30^m 30^s per annum for the last 50 or 60 years in this part of the country.

Great change in the leaves, dead ones falling all around us, and the others all becoming yellow. Continued struggling and cutting our way through the swamp without finding water, the men working without their dinners are discontented. Wilkinson appearing to have made a false estimate of the distance to the S.W. branch of the Saint John, and night coming on with the men separated and the luggage and provisions far behind, I was obliged to desist and encamp in a damp part of the swamp. Sent Wilkinson to direct the men to bring up provisions &c for the night. Most fortunately they got in just at dark. In the meantime my son and myself prepared the camping ground and spruce boughs to lay over the wet ground. Having got our fires built, and old Peter having discovered a little water, we got some supper and laid down.

Saturday, October 12th. Very cold night. Before we went to bed, a gun was heard in the direction of Lake Kiaquagam [Caucomgomuc Lake]. We fired twice in return, but hearing no further from the other party, some of our people thought it must have been a straggling hunter, although I still adhere to the opinion that it was a signal from Col. M's party, yesterday being the day agreed upon for our meeting in this neigbourhood.

Up at daybreak this morning and roused the hands; sent some out to finish cutting the road to the Saint John River and others to bring up one of the birch canoes. Fired a gun at 1/2 past 8 a.m. but no answer. Fahr. at 8, 30°, bright morning. After breakfast walked to the Saint John about the 8th of a mile from our camp. A very pretty cheerful stream, rather too shallow to ascend very high. About 15 feet wide and very dry pretty banks. Cut the initials of our young Queen on a beautiful white birch on the right bank of the stream. Excellent land around, this will make a good farming country.

At 1/4 before 1 p.m. got once more into my canoe, and very much pleased with the change, being wearied out with tramping about in swamps and bogs, and sleeping on the wet ground. Again James and myself go gliding downstream, very crooked, the general course however about North. The water is low and evidently impenetrable higher up to the South. In 1 1/2 miles came into more still and deep water, occasioned by the setting back of the lake.

About 2 p.m., the water being about 5 deep, the channel crooked, my son, with Nadeau and old Peter in the canoe, old Peter in the bow, we suddenly came upon a cow moose walking in the river; she had one or two calves in the brushwood on the right bank which I heard but did not see. James saw one of them. The cow began to swim downstream, apparently with the intention of alluring us from her young, and old Peter with his eyes in fire and full of anxiety and animation took his gun and snapped the trigger as she was attempting to get up a steep bank. The gun missed and I handed him his powder horn when he fired with effect. We saw the blood stream from her and that she faltered. Peter now desired us to stop and advance further, saying she would die and indeed if we had gone near her in her dying struggle she would have crushed our frail machine in an instant. It was a distressing scene to witness her death, she rose and fell repeatedly in the water, and at last came upon her back and made the most violent exertions before she died. When she was motionless we turned her to the left bank and dragged her ashore when Peter opened her paunch to prevent the meat spoiling from the putrefying gas in her entrails. Having done this we pursued our way to the lake through a deep stream about 150 feet wide. Near the mouth we met two Saint John Indians, acquaintances of Peter, who had arrived the evening before and had no information to give us of Col. Mudge's party.

On reaching the lake a little before 3 p.m. and examining it around with a telescope, we saw no smoke and no signs of the party. I therefore engaged the two Indians to go to our portage and bring my servant and McQueen with our cooking apparatus, upon condition of giving them some biscuits, giving Peter permission to go and skin his moose. The killing of this moose gave me pain. I would not have shot her myself, having a great repugnance to kill animals of any sort, and it would be impossible for me to shoot at a cow or anything like one. But we have been fortunate in falling in with her since Col. Mudge has failed bringing us supplies. This animal has a monstrous long head like a camel, with a large flexible upper lip to get the leaves with. She also resembles a large mule, being of a grey colour with a skin resembling one, a reddish grey. The ears are a mixture of those of the ass and deer, the legs are graceful and very perfect small hoofs. She had a pretty bag of milk and was by no means thin. I think she would weigh 350 lbs. Whilst she was retreating before us in the water, her head somewhat resembled that of a rhinoceros. Peter says he has twice seen a cow moose with 3 calves. He also says he has at various times heard the morning and evening gun at Quebec, the air being perfectly still. This is a great distance, Quebec being I suppose 80 miles from [Baker Lake], where he was at the time. The lake is a tame but pleasing piece of water about 3 miles long and perhaps 1 mile across. The land rises a little from the shore, but not much.

The leaves are all embrowned and in another week there will not be one left. The mud on the shores of the stream as we came down this afternoon was covered with impressions of the hoofs of the moose across the wide southern beach of the lake. The two Indians who arrived here yesterday killed two in the course of the day, and have killed 16 within a very short time. A little after dark the Indians returned with my servant, the evening threatens to be stormy. With our tent nicely strewed with boughs we supped on some trout and laid down.

Sunday, October 13th. Rain at night, succeeded by high wind, W.N.W. The non-appearance of Col. Mudge is an embarrassing affair. He selected to come with the provisions, and especially agreed to meet me here on the 10th day, whilst today is the 13th, and there is no intelligence of him. All my provision is exhausted and if the weather had been inclement, as it well might have been at this season, and we had not had the good fortune to kill the moose yesterday, my camp would have been starving. As it is I cannot investigate further in this direction, and our common safety obliges me to draw towards the North, to be near some quarter where supplies may be drawn. Col. M. must be well aware of the difficulty of my position; I explained most particularly to him that the safety of my party depended upon his bringing me supplies, and that it was through those supplies alone I would be enabled to traverse the chain I have discovered to the S.W. Besides I have no longer the means to transport my party, having been obliged to abandon our big log canoes, and now we have only two birch barks left to convey the six men and the various objects left behind. Regrets are useless paid. I must extricate my party as well as I can. What is excessively vexatious is that all the opportunities of making observations at this interesting point are lost, the importance of which it is impossible to make the Col. conscious of. So much for selecting men to execute an enterprise requiring the greatest energy & experience, who have neither one nor the other.

At 20 m. past 11 a.m. left the camp and taking one of the Indians with me, went up the river to our old camp at the end of our portage. Our store for this investigation here being broken up, having only 16 lbs pork, 30 lbs biscuits, about 1 lb of tea and no sugar left, I instructed Wilkinson to return down the Saint John as soon as the men had brought up the two canoes, and to leave them at their homes, giving him a check for £200 to pay their wages, dividing the few provisions we had given to him. I bade this faithful and intelligent man adieu and regained my own camp. I have now engaged the two Indians and their canoe to go with me as far as Mittagwakis, to take McQueen, Parsons, the instruments and other objects. From thence if I see no more of Col. M. I shall proceed as well as I can to Quebec, and from thence go to the Metis [Rivière Mitis], after examining the nature of the highlands which the Americans chose to be the boundary.

Purchased the horns and head skin of a young moose of one of the Indians of whom I got the head of a *loup-cervier*, or lynx, which the people of Maine call lucifee. At 2 p.m. loaded our canoes, which being top heavy, could not contain the moose meat, this we left at the lake shore for Wilkinson to take. We were obliged to proceed with much caution, sending Parsons, McQueen and the instruments with the two Indians by the lake shore, that if they upset nothing might be lost.

From the N. end of the lake had a fine view of the range of mountains I ascended on the 7th Oct. We reached the N. end of [Baker Lake] in 50 minutes; it is probably 3 1/2 miles long, the outlet we found rocky and shallow, the waters being low through all the water courses. About 1/2 a mile from the lake we met Hansard's party. They had been detained by the shallowness of the Saint John and by their indolent movements. Col. M. was still unshaven, looking most wretchedly. He never made one inquiry about what I had seen, where I had been, or what results I had reached. His total apathy is inconceivable. I have no doubt he has not taken a single observation of any kind since we parted. His mind is now full of going to Quebec. We stopped to encamp on the right bank about 1/2 past 4 p.m. Here, having built my fire and supped, I retired to rest as early as I could.

Monday, October 14th. Cloudy morning, rose at 6 a.m., had my camp fire renewed. Despatched Alex Burgoyne with a canoe and letter to Wilkinson, to assist him to transport his party. Directed him to transport all my luggage from the Grand Falls to Fredericton. Went to Col. Mudge's camp; it appears now that he mistakenly directed Mr. Maclauchlan to send his luggage to Quebec if we did not return to Sir John Caldwell's by the 10th October, as if it had been under any circumstances possible for us to be at the Grand Falls by that time, or any time near it, and I am now afraid that Maclauchlan has mistaken him and sent mine also. It is evident Col. Mudge does not intend to return to F'ton, although he conceals it from me. I have thought it prudent to tell him this morning that our instructions direct our bills of exchange to be signed by both, and that they will not be paid unless so signed. His answer was, "We must see to provide against that." How this is to be done without going to F'ton and finding how much they amount to,

I am not able to conceive. In two or three days we shall arrive at the Etchemin portage and some determination will have to be come to. I learn that Col. M. thinks to evade the necessity of going to F'ton by authorizing someone by power of attorney to sign the bills for him. Even supposing this to be satisfactory to the Foreign Office, the accounts will still remain to be settled, a ceremony that remains to be gone through and which for my own security must be efficiently done before we part, for I perceive every reason to apprehend that Col. M. means to leave me the first opportunity in order to get to Quebec & Montreal, and that he will embark for England without giving a further thought to me or to the expedition.

The worst trait in his character is selfishness, all his movements are the result of that degrading feeling. A circumstance has occurred illustrative of this. Before we left F'ton he heard of a quantity of preserved French dishes and vegetables which an officer had brought over and had not used. M. directed Wilkinson our commissary to purchase them. When I dismissed the men at the 4th Lake, it was necessary to send back everything that was superfluous to lighten our canoes as all superfluities increase the weight of our burden, both on the water and especially on the portages, where everything being to be carried on men's backs, increased materially the expense of the expedition by obliging us to employ additional men. These preserved meats, with brandy and other things not in any manner necessary to us, I directed to be sent back to F'ton and delivered them over to Morrison who had charge of the return party, taking a receipt from him for them. I now learn that after my back was fairly turned, Col. M. sent a canoe after Morrison's party for the very articles I had sent off, and that he has been feasting upon them ever since. Instead of coming to my relief within the ten days, knowing I must be in want of everything, he has hastened away the time in personal indulgences of eating, drinking and sleeping. This morning after I was washed, shaved and dressed and ready, I passed him in bed. At 1/2 past 7 a.m. his party was not ready, and I finally came away leaving them behind mending M's canoe, all of which should have been done before 8 a.m.

The water continues very shallow and the fall of the country very great. Peter says when he came down this river six years ago in the spring, it was so high that the current was too rapid; indeed upon such occasions the velocity owing to the great fall must be very great. At present we have to haul the canoe along the bed of the river for the first 3 miles, there being only about 3 inches of water. We have not made more than 3/4 of a mile an hour. At 1/2 past 1 p.m. came to deadish water, when halted to give the men a morsel to eat. At 1/2 past 2 p.m., having dried my shoes and stockings, we proceeded dragging the canoe another mile and a half when came to dead water, in a low marshy part of the country which has been an ancient lake. Here we paddled 5 miles and at 1/2 past 4 p.m. I stopped near an open plain on the right bank where a stream comes in to camp, in order to give Col. Mudge an opportunity of coming up with us. I built him a fire and cleared him a camping place near to ours. About 8 p.m. I fired a gun, but receiving no answer, I gave up the hope of his joining us tonight. We passed 2 small streams joining the river from the right bank, one about 5 1/2 miles from the lake, the other 10 miles: and one small stream coming in on the left bank, about 6 miles from the lake. The course of today was nearly N., a few degrees to the W. sometimes. To bed at 1/2 past 8.

Tuesday, October 15th. Rose early. It appears my party has brought away all the pork and bed clothes of Col. M's party, and that their party has got the tea and sugar. These are the consequences of moving so irregularly through the country. I am now obliged to wait the arrival of Col. M., throwing away all this precious time, which ought to be employed in examining those important affairs concerning the American line of highlands. Soon we shall have the winter upon us. It is a remarkable fact that Col. M., during the whole period we were together yesterday, never made the slightest inquiry concerning the results of my lake excursion to the Penobscot waters. The man's mind is fairly resolved as respects the great object of our expedition.

Peter says it is about 15 miles from hence to the Mittaywaquam [Daaquam River], that it is 15 miles westward to the forks of that stream, passing a branch trending northwards called Eesheeganilsaghee [Rivière aux Orignaux], meaning rock on one side and grassy swamp on the other. Taking the left hand branch of the forks, it is 9 miles to the portage which leads to Lake Etchemin; on these last 9 miles you cross Major Yule's line of railroad.[46] From the portage 12 miles to Lake Etchemin, so that we are 51 miles to Lake Etchemin.

One o'clock p.m. I have waited with as much patience as I could assume to this hour and Col. M. does not appear. It is evident he has not stirred from his encampment of yesterday. How he can excuse this delay to himself, this loss of precious time and this unprofitable expense of detaining the whole party I cannot conceive. If his canoe even was unfit for further service, why not come down in Hansard's canoe and leave the party behind to join Wilkinson. He knows the importance of making use of every moment of time to get to the Mitis, that the waters are falling fast every day, and that the delay must throw me into the winter. I am provoked almost beyond endurance. I shall certainly come to a full explanation with him and push on to the Mitis whether he goes or not. If he chooses to trifle with the service he must be responsible. I exert myself to the extent of my power, am up late and early, and will not share the blame unfairly, belonging to the indolence and indifference of another man. This is a beautiful day and he is altogether inexcusable if he has neglected to make observations for latitude and variation.

At 3 p.m. Col. M. arrived with Wilkinson's party; the reason assigned for the delay, mending the birch canoes. My canoe has always been examined the last thing at night, and necessary repairs made before starting in the morning.

We now pursued our course N. down the Saint John on dead water about 5 miles when shoal water commenced, and it wanting only 1/2 an hour to night I encamped that the men might not get wet tonight as they will probably have to be all day tomorrow. Going over to Col. M's camp, I spoke to him of the pernicious effects of these delays, of the absolute necessity of our being on the water early and late, on account of the rapid falling of the water, and asked as a favour of him that he would have his party turned out early in the morning, as it was my determination not to delay my movements an instant. His answer was singularly ingenuous, that he never interfered in anything, that he always waited until he was

---

46 Major Patrick Yule, R.E. (1792-1873), a versatile and much travelled officer who, in 1838, published a pamphlet on the disputed boundary.

told all was ready, being always ready for the moment. A singular answer; leaving the men to their own movements, who never stir without rousing, and always delay their departure as long as they can, to prolong their ease, shorten their day's work, and get more wages. It was equivalent to saying he "let the men do just as they pleased".

I next asked him about his intentions, told him that the information he had given me of having ordered his luggage to Quebec had made it necessary I should take my own measures, as I was determined to proceed to the Mitis. Here he gave me an answer, as singular as the first, that it was absolutely necessary that he as a military man should go to Montreal to see Sir John Colborne,[47] the Commander in Chief, who was not apprised even that we were in his district. I told him the Marquis of Normanby[48] had informed him officially of the fact, and that he knew we were the bearers of a letter of introduction to him, but that Sir John had nothing to do with us, nor we with him, except we were casually where he was to be seen, that the completion of our instructions were our real business, and that he knew he must be at Fredericton with me to sign the bills of exchange which would not be paid unless signed as our instructions directed. He then said he would sign blank bills of exchange, and after a further conversation I agreed to accompany him to Quebec if it was possible to get through the country there, and take the blank bills. I saw he had already taken his measures, had ordered his luggage there, and was determined to go, and dreading lest he should leave me in the lurch with all the bills to pay upon my own responsibility, and that I should have to draw upon Mr. Stavely[49] upon my simple authority, and contrary to my instructions, I thought it better, as I had some official business at Quebec, to go with him, and thus avoid everything being thrown into inextricable confusion at the final liquidation of the accounts. My measures therefore are now to be taken accordingly and I have thought it prudent to commit to my notebook all the details of his conduct and our conversation, that the true reasons of what may appear irregular in our proceedings may appear, and I myself be held blameless. It is impossible for me to control him; I am not his superior, and if I were I could not do it, as he appears to be insensible to a responsibility which weighs me down with anxiety. I regret all this, for at bottom I think Col. M. an amiable person; a selfish apprehensiveness seems to govern him and everything is subordinate with him to his own personal safety and comfort. Having supped and given Wilkinson instructions, I laid down at 9 p.m.

Wednesday, October 16th. A fine morning. Up early, shaved and dressed, and had everyone up preparing their breakfast and canoes for departure. Left our camp at 10 m. after 8 a.m. Tolerable water for the first hour, when the shoals

---

47 Sir John Colborne, first Baron Seaton (1778-1863). A former lieutenant-governor of Upper Canada, he was served in that office by Mudge's younger brother Zachariah (1800-31), in the capacity of private secretary.

48 Constantine Henry Phipps (1797-1863), 1st Marquess of Normanby, British Secretary of State for War and the Colonies, February to August 1839.

49 Thomas Stavely, of the Foreign Office.

began and we had to drag our canoes, almost without intermission until noon when, the men tired, stopped at noon of their own accord to light a fire for their dinners. As it had been a severe morning and they were on their return I did not oppose it.

A bad leak in my canoe made mę wet through, made myself a fire by the bank of the river and dried my shoes and stockings. A warm day and a brilliant sun. Col. M. went afishing when I hoped to see him occupied with taking an observation for altitude, but I shall say no more to him, and get through as well as I can.

At 1/2 past 1 p.m. resumed our course, in 20 m. we passed the Wayukten-mahteek in the S.W. branch of the Saint John. It is a fine stream about 100 feet wide, of the size of the S.E. branch. The river after the junction becomes about 200 feet wide, inclines to the N.E. and affords much better navigation. The distance from this fork to the next, or [Daaquam], is said to be 8 miles, the Wayuktenmahteek taking its rise in the lofty hills where the branches of the Metgermette, a branch of the Chaudière, rises. The River Saint John for the rest of the afternoon keeps about a N.E. course, exactly parallel with the stratification as I observed the strata trending with the river. The banks of the Saint John are richly studded with the *sorbus americana* [American mountain ash], the fruit of which is now ripe and of the richest colour. We had a beautiful afternoon, worked hard myself using the paddle in order to arrive at the forks and make our arrangements. Passed Chase's Stream on our right, and at 3 p.m. came to [Daaquam], a broad looking tributary on our left. Here on a point at its mouth on the N. side, near a portage cut out by Major Yule, we stopped to encamp.

Half an hour afterwards Col. M. arrived. Being desirous of making all the arrangements for the new party going to Quebec, I sent to ask him to my tent and showed him my plan for taking up three canoes. He objected to it and said if he could not have what he deemed comfortable he would have it and pay for it out of his own pocket. He also meant to take Hearnden the sapper, partly he said to act as his orderly, and because he was desirous of verifying the barometers and taking an observation at Lake Champlain. As I perceived it was all to gratify his vanity, I said nothing, but said he should have an extra canoe. Mr. Hansard expressed a wish to go to Quebec. As he could be of no use to the public service, I objected to increasing the expense as he would want a canoe and man, when he very properly said that he wished to go at his own personal expense, and as he is a well-meaning man who has been of some use I agreed to forward him to Etchemin. Mr. Wilkinson came to make arrangements about the ultimate disposition of everything going down the Saint John, a matter causing a great deal of calculation and trouble and expense, all of which could have been avoided by Col. M's accompanying me to Madawaska, even if he had not gone to the Mitis. Laid down at 9 p.m.

Thursday, October 17th. Beautiful morning, had everything packed for our expedition. After breakfast got the party organized and despatched the canoes; myself & my son, Mr. Hansard and the two sappers proceeding by land on a portage of 7 miles cut by Major Yule along the banks of the stream to the first branch of the [Daaquam]. A pleasant walk, numerous tracks of moose, low but good farming land. On arriving at the fork found old Peter waiting for me, but Col. M. and the other canoes not arrived. Found some bark wigwams at the point of the junction made by Major Yule's party. Directed the men to cook their dinners. Reached the fork at 1 p.m. The [Daaquam] is a wide stream of 100 feet wide with much more water than either of the great southern branches of the Willastan. After dinner Col. M., my son and others walked to the western termination of Major Yule's portage, about 3 1/2 miles. I came in my canoe, handsome stream and excellent poling. Halted for the night a few minutes before 5 p.m. on the right bank. Small trees for fuel. Got our supper at 7 p.m. and laid down.

Friday, October 18th. Rose at 6 a.m. and hastened the party that we might get a part of the Etchemin portage made today. Mild warm morning like yesterday, Fahr. 47°. Breakfasted and left the camp a few minutes before 8 a.m., enjoining the others to follow immediately. Found good poling with few exceptions. At 12 m, having reached the forks, 10 miles, left the main [Daaquam] on the right and entered the branch on the left, all dead water. Stopped near this and lighted a fire for the men to cook by. Waited here in vain until Col. M. and his party came up which was not until 2 p.m., they having loitered on the way and stopped to cook, leaving us without provisions, and losing the precious time, a matter of infinitely more importance. On my rating Hansard with this trifling conduct, he answered that he was not to blame, that Col. M. had "desired he should not go before him." Col. M. told me he had waited for the rest, but everything seems secondary to preceding everybody on the river to get a shot at a wild duck. Thus by an improper waste of time we shall defeat all my arrangements, shall not arrive at the portage tonight and thus probably be prevented getting over L. Etchemin and have to sleep without tents or bedding. They will then suffer for their inconsiderate conduct.

Pushed on for the portage, made about 8 miles, and night coming on were obliged to stop in a swampy country. On my pointing all this out to Col. M., he answered, "Yes, it is a pity." Got our fire built up at a swampy place as well as we could, and laid down.

Saturday, October 19th. Rose before daylight and had the fire made, breakfasted, had our packages made up for the portage and got into our canoes. Reached the portage and, having strapped the baggage to the men's shoulders, began our march of 12 miles, through bogs and swamps and part of the way firm land. James and myself did not stop on the road but made the distance at the rate of one mile for every 26 minutes. Col. M. arrived exactly 2 hours after. Changed my clothes for dry ones.

Nadeau, having made a small raft, crossed the lake three miles and returned with a large bateau and a man, got all our party into it and crossed Lake Etchemin. Snow began to fall. Stopped at the Farmers of the Commissary General who has an establishment here. Candish the farmer, a Scotchman, was in Quebec. His wife rec^d us rather coolly, but gave us supper. At 8 p.m. the man arrived from Quebec and rec^d us very coolly. It appears they had been informed we were Yankees, as they said, come to take possession, but being satisfied who we were, they behaved with great hospitality and spread beds for us on the floor! By the

Quebec papers I learnt that Poulett Thomson[50] had reached Quebec as Governor General. We heard the cannon firing this afternoon on reaching the lake.

Sunday, October 20th. Frost with some snow, rose early, got a hearty breakfast. Made arrangements for our journey to Quebec. Left the lake about 8 a.m., with four carts, two with the luggage and the others for those who chose to ride through the most wretched rocky and swampy roads imaginable. Choosing to walk, I left the carts to the others. Passed the Etchemin River and took the elevation by barometer on the bridge, a mile further took the elevation on the crest of the ridge, this being part of the chain the Americans claim for their Highlands. This chain is about 20 m. wide, running N.E. & S.W., has some lofty peaks but is not connected with the true highlands; there is a chasm of at least 30 miles between them. It runs parallel with the St. Lawrence, connecting itself on the other side of the Chaudière with its western continuation. I must examine this subject more in detail at Quebec at the Surveyor General's office. Passed the [Ruisseau à l'Eau-Chaude], so called because it does not freeze in the winter, whilst it is the coldest brook in the country in the summer. At 8 m. from L. Etchemin a settlement of poor Irish people in a pretty country, the hills sloping down to fine bottom lands through which the pretty Etchemin flows.

At 15 miles, having walked the whole way, stopped at a store kept by one Wilson, a hypocritical rascal who pretended he had nothing in the house, and that at any rate he would sell nothing on a Sunday. Having at length produced rum & biscuit, which I gave to the men, and asking him what was to pay, he said half a dollar. I left him in disgust, continuing my journey on foot with my son. Col. M. continued to ride through all this hard road with his buffalo skins on, making the strangest appearance, everyone staring at him. We told them he was the American warden of the disputed territory whom we had taken prisoner.

Having reached Mr. Henderson's 18 miles from the lake, near the bridge across the Etchemin, and being very much fatigued with my long walk and very foot sore, I called in and introduced myself, where he and his lady kindly gave me some good bread and butter to eat, with excellent milk, and lent me his cart and horse to go to Ste-Claire. I reached this place at evening, very cold, wet in the feet, and in some pain. Here I found my son who had walked 25 miles, waiting in the street not knowing how far to proceed. We warmed ourselves at a Canadian's where I saw two very pretty children, twins, and pursuing our journey in a cold moonlight evening, reached Venner's at St-Anselme, 30 m. from the lake. Venner is an old soldier in the 1st Dragoon Guards who was in the action where General Brock was killed in 1812.[51] Being disbanded he married a Canadian and keeps a good country tavern. Here we got a plentiful supper and retired to bed at 10 p.m., worn out with fatigue and suffering in my bleeding feet.

Monday, October 21st. Rose at 7 a.m., washed my feet which are in a bad state, and after breakfast got into our carts and started for Quebec, 18 miles. Very bad

---

50 Charles Edward Poulett Thomson, first Baron Sydenham (1799-1841), Governor General of Canada, 1839-41.

51 Sir Isaac Brock (1769-1812), died at Queenston Heights.

roads the greatest part of the way. A little past 2 p.m. arrived at Point Levis, having had a fine view of the Citadel and town with the shipping on coming down the hill. The highlands I used to look at with Lord Durham from the Government House last year at this time are the highlands the Americans claim as the true line. We had a well-defined view of them at various points, and the statement I gave in to Government about the interval between those highlands and the highlands north of the St. Lawrence turned out to be correct, as I convinced Col. M. That interval is the old bed of the St. Lawrence.

At Quebec got into comfortable quarters at the Albion, Sir John Colborne occupying my old ones at Payne's. Col. Campbell of the Artillery called and said Sir John would be delighted to see us and that he was talking of me yesterday. Got an excellent dinner at 1/2 past 5 p.m., just before which Col. Ashburnham of the Coldstream Guards called and asked me to dine tomorrow, which I was obliged to decline, having no clothes and sore feet. Went to bed at 8.

Tuesday, October 22nd. Arose at 7, somewhat refreshed, dressed and came to a comfortable fire in our parlour. After breakfast got some moccasins for my sore feet, and with Col. Mudge called on the new Governor General, Cha⁵ Poulett Thomson, who received us pleasantly. We had a long conversation with him about the disputed territory and then called upon Sir John Colborne whom I had not seen since 1829. Had a long conversation with him. He introduced me to Sir Rd Jackson,[52] the new Commander in Chief. Saw my old acquaintance Sir James Macdonell[53] and others. Came to my lodgings and commenced our Despatch No. 4 to Lord Palmerston. Wrote various letters to go by the *Pique* frigate which sails tomorrow with Sir John Colborne on her return to England. Dined at 5 p.m. and continued writing until 9 when retired.

Wednesday, October 23rd. A cloudy but mild morning. Finished my despatches and letters, and took them to the Post Office. Called on Sir John Colborne and took leave. Saw the guard escort him to the quay. Made various calls and purchases. Mr. W. Price went with me to the Bank of British North America, and engaged to procure me some blank bills of exchange. Capt. Stewart of the *Ringdove* offered me a passage down the river tomorrow at 8 a.m. Wrote to ask him if he could delay it until Friday. Was kind enough to call and agreed to wait. Dined at our hotel and went to bed at 10 p.m.

Thursday, October 24th. A heavy storm of thunder & lightning in the night. The claps were tremendously loud and shook the house. After breakfast wrote to Mr. Fox about the existing condition of the disputed territory. Had a long conversation with Sir James McDonell on the same subject of which he made a note to transmit to Sir R. Jackson. At 5 p.m. drove to Mr. Price's to dinner where met Col. Bowly, Col. Ashburnham, Col. Codrington and other gentlemen. Mrs. P. looked

---

52 Lieutenant-General Sir Richard Downes Jackson (1777-1845), administrator of the government of Lower Canada, 1839-40.

53 General Sir James Macdonell (d.1857), a hero of Waterloo and chosen by Wellington for the award as bravest man in the British Army.

as pretty as ever. Capt. K. Stewart who was there gave me until 9 a.m. tomorrow to go on board the *Ringdove* with my party. Came away at 11 p.m. Mr. Price very kindly giving me letters to his agents at Rimouski to assist me in my operations at the Mitis.

Friday, October 25th. Rose very early and having breakfasted and got everything ready, left the hotel and Col. M. at 1/2 past 8 a.m. and went to the Queen's wharf where the *Ringdove*'s boat came and took us on board. The Hon. Capt. K. Stewart received me in the most friendly manner, and made me as comfortable as he could in his small cabin, being much amused with the change from the woods to a man of war. After an excellent dinner, Mr. Grey, one of the lieutenants, and Mr. Harris another officer, being present, turned in to my berth. We came to anchor about 2 p.m., a/c of calm.

Saturday, October 26th. Rose at 7 a.m., found we were under weigh with an aft wind. Made an excellent breakfast and set my son to copy an official letter to the Gov. General. Mr. Shepherd & Mr. Tarleton dined with us today, the latter is a very intelligent young officer. All the officers appear to be very amiable and clever men. At dark came to an anchor at the Brandy Pots, opposite to Rivière-du-Loup, the wind ... dying away and the Captain not daring to trust to the tides, there being a crooked navigation here and no anchorage until you reach Bic. Went to bed at 9 p.m.

Sunday, October 27th. Fog and calm. Still at anchor off the Brandy Pots. After breakfast went to the officers' gun room and main deck by invitation. She is a very roomy nice brig and they appear to be very happy on board. The men are fine looking fellows and appear very cheerful. Fahr. ther. 45°, a pleasant but calm day. About noon landed at the Brandy Pots Island. Rocks running N.E. & S.W., strong beds of conglomerate pebbles, slate & quartz, beds of calcareous matter with cavities resembling organic substances containing cubes of pyrites. A great many berries on the island, cranberries, blueberries and the fruit of the sorbus. Capt. Stewart and the doctor shot a couple of rabbits. It was calm when we landed, and after rambling an hour and a half, a strong westerly wind sprung up and made a rather high sea.

Had a hard pull with four young sailors to reach the brig, the motion made me rather sick, the waves running high. At 1/2 past 3 p.m. dined by invitation with the officers in the gun room. Having got under weigh on returning on board, and the wind lulling a good deal, we came abreast Green Island [L'Isle Verte] about 1/2 past 5 p.m. Wind lulling, I turned in having no further expectation of landing until tomorrow morning.

Monday, October 28th. Foul wind E.N.E. and wet morning. Brig beating down upon Bic Island [Ile du Bic] to land me. Made a hearty breakfast with the captain whose kind attentions to me have quite attached me to him. At 10 a.m. took leave of the captain's officers, stepped into the pilot boat and steered for Old Bic, distant about 10 miles. Sea tolerably high and pilot boat heeling quite enough to make the shoregoing people feel uncomfortable. In 2 hours we apprehended the shore and found it impossible to land, owing to the state of the tide, being low water, the pilot too obstinately refusing to risk his boat being injured, saying it was all he had in the world. McQueen waded up to the middle ashore, being excessively cold, and took a man ashore on his shoulders who sent us down a cart, by the aid of which we landed and got to a dirty cottage of Canadians amongst the rocks and mud, who furnished us with two caleches. At 2 p.m. we started for Rimouski, 10 miles, passing a great many cottages and snug Canadian farms until we arrived at Rimouski River. Here we left the caleches and crossed the ferry to Capt. Gardner's to whom Mr. W. Price had given me a letter. Learnt he was at Mitis. Mrs. G. rec'd us, offered us beds. 5 little daughters, 1 infant son. Got a very indifferent repast of stale bread and tough pork, and went to bed about 9 p.m

Tuesday, October 29th. Up early, rainy weather still. Got an indifferent breakfast; at 9 a.m. started in 2 caleches for the River Mitis. Called on Mr. Gauvreau the post master and left a despatch for the Gov. General. He invited me to sleep at his house on my return. Had a very pleasant ride along the St. Lawrence. The beach at low water is very broad, formed by blue slates occasionally red, running E.N.E. and gravel. Immense numbers of dead shells nearby, mussels and of the pholas kind. The lands appear good as far as the high banks which are variously from one to five hundred yards from the water. They are neatly farmed by Canadians, their white houses and barns being usually painted white, or whitewashed, and no dirt about them.

About 8 miles from Rimouski is a neat settlement of pilots called Pointe-au-Père. One mile before reaching Mitis, the road stops and we had to cross a bay about one mile, nearly up to the horse's belly. At high water this bay is impassable, and travellers only proceed at low water. At the end of this mile came to the mouth of the Mitis. Called at Mr. MacNider's, the Seigneur of the lands here, who received us kindly, gave us a good dinner of excellent trout and English ale. Engaged two Indians with their canoes to proceed with us tomorrow. Walked to their settlement on the Matapédia road; they are few in number.

Wednesday, October 30th. Cold thick morning. The brother of this Mr. MacNider acquired this seigniory by purchase and left it to his two sons. The youngest here is a very excellent and intelligent man, does not appear to be more than 17 years old, yet manages everything very well. The seigniory is principally settled by Scotch and Irish families, some of whom live 4 or 5 miles back in the country. Having caused a young beeve to be killed for our provisions, bread to be baked and some other preparations, about 1/2 past 11 a.m. we sent off a cart with these things and some blankets the MacNiders lent us, and getting into a caleche set off to where our canoes were, about 6 miles off.

A wretched road in a swampy forest. About 3 miles off we turned down on foot thro' the woods to look at a very interesting cataract upon the Mitis. The bed of the river here is about 100 yards wide, and in the spring the water falls about 100 feet over the whole breadth, at present the water being low, and the stream only about 50 feet wide, the rest of the bed shows the slates in their schistose lamina N.E. & S.W., dipping about 45° S.E. It is a beautiful sheet, falling in a column to the bottom, with a small projection towards the top. Having sent back our caleche we continued from hence on foot to Le Mercier's, one of our men, where we were to embark. The river is very crooked and the alluvial borders very wide, giving excessive flats occasionally of 100 acres. We passed one clearing of about 50 acres, very well prepared for next year by a number of Canadians.

Le Mercier's cabin stands in this clearing on the banks of the river here about 80 feet wide. He is a stout Canadian who has been almost brought up amongst the Micmacs whose tongue he speaks perfectly. He has a squaw for his wife, extremely plain and apparently much older than him. They have two young daughters, the eldest about 14, both of them pleasing and rather graceful girls, very Indian in complexion and features, yet softened down by their Canadian blood. We found a very good looking and clever Canadian woman, his sister, 27 years old. She had come all the way from Quebec this autumn on a visit to her brother who had been absent from his family 23 years, and was going to stay the winter. She was cheerful, said it was a curious *ménage,* but she had not been *ennuyée* in 3 months she had been there.

1/4 before 3 p.m. entered our canoes and poled vigorously upstream. The river has a strong current but a good stream to pole on. The weather as usual dark, foggy, and rather wet, as it has been ever since the 27th Oct. At 1/4 past 4 p.m. stopped and made our camp on a low place on the right bank. No white birch bark here. Filled in the back of our camp with spruce which is good here. Made a hearty repast and about 1/2 past 7 laid down to rest.

Thursday, October 31st. Got very little sleep last night, although I was warm. Le Mercier went back to his house last night for a pot to boil their meat in, having neglected to bring one. These Canadians and Indians are very improvident; Noël our head man has not even brought a blanket with him. He says his wife has two but refused to give him one of them; he therefore has nothing but the fire to keep him warm.

Another dull drizzling morning. Breakfasted about 1/2 past 7 a.m. At 1/2 past 8 a.m. left our camp. Strong current and hard poling, snow falling until past 11. After which a steady small rain until night. Had to take our bread out of the bag to dry it when the men stopped at 1/2 past 12 to eat. Started again at 2 p.m. and went on in the rain, struggling against a rapid current until 1/2 past 4 p.m. when stopped to encamp. Made a very comfortable shanty with poles and birch bark, got our fire agoing, our clothes dried, and having made a comfortable supper laid down to rest.

Friday, November 1st. Up a little after 6 a.m., snowing but mild weather. Hastened the breakfast and at 1/4 past 8 a.m. got the men into the canoes and, the stream being rapid and shallow, James, myself and Parsons walked. Got wet through very soon, the ground being covered with soft snow and the trees and bushes dripping water like rain. At 3 miles, stopped at the right bank, lit a fire, and one of the canoes coming up, changed myself. Continued struggling with the rapids and shoals until 1/4 past 12 m. where all hands being fatigued, stopped to dine and give them an opportunity of drying themselves and mending the canoes. The slates here are less fissile and in some places almost horizontal; the cause of this, as I [found] afterwards, is their occasional anticlinal structure.

Our Indian Noël and his Canadian Le Mercier do not deserve the great character Mr. MacNider gave them. The Canadian is a boasting, talkative fellow, of more words than actions. His canoe which he praised so much and urged me to buy for four louis is a very poor one, badly made, leaks, and he is so insolent as to threaten to leave us if we don't walk in the woods. I ordered him to take Parsons & McQueen on board, which he did with reluctance, but put them on shore the moment I was out of sight, and they arrived worn out at the camp when nearly dark. Noël is always refusing to do something or other lest he should break his canoe, and I only keep them in a state of imperfect obedience by threatening not to pay them anything.

We had a very severe afternoon, the stream was very rapid, the ledges of rock crossed it every 1/4 of a mile at right angles, and obliged us to force our canoe, in which myself and son were, up a sort of cataract repeatedly. At 1/4 past 4 p.m., all exhausted, we stopped for the night on the left bank and got our camp up, supped and laid down. N.B. We left a quarter of beef hanging on a tree at 2 p.m. to lighten our load.

Saturday, November 2nd. Passed a very indifferent night, sleeping very little and the snow falling so in my face that I was compelled to cover my head with the blanket. Got up to warm myself at 1/4 past 6 a.m. and washed and dressed. Morning thick as usual. Got afloat at 8 a.m., my son and the two men walking as usual. River almost impassable for a canoe, quite furious; at length came to a ledge of rocks 8 feet high which effectually stopped us. Here we made a portage of a 1/4 of a mile, then proceeded 1 1/2 miles to a cataract of about 25 feet where made a portage of about 1 mile crossing a high ridge, at the South end of this portage made fires and cooked dinner for the Indians whilst they brought the canoes across &c. My son took the barometrical height whilst I attended to the important duty of drying the bread which had again got wet.

At 1/2 past 12 p.m. proceeded for 1/2 a mile and the rapids becoming impassable, we made another portage of 1/4 of a mile. At the end of this discovered we had broken a hole at the bottom of my canoe, obliged to make a fire, insert a new piece of bark and pay it with pitch. The river now became more manageable and the country looked as if we were approaching a flat lake country. At 1/4 past 4 p.m. stopped for the night, wet and fatigued. Got into an indifferent country for fuel and boughs, but at length got up a fire, dried our feet and got our camp fixed in a wet mossy land. My head ached and I felt unwell. McQueen has a violent cold, and we are all tired enough of the discomfort we continually experience. Got some supper and laid down.

Sunday, November 3rd. Passed a very poor night; hard and damp ground, and seldom able to get asleep. The fire caught the men's bed clothes and burnt the rugs and blankets. Rose at 6 a.m., glad to rise, had the fire mended, breakfast cooked and everything ready for our departure. Our miserable Indians, who never have anything when it was wanted, who take no pitch or bark when they leave their wigwams, altho' sure they will want them, and who carry no paddles altho' they know they must have them, have now to waste my precious time by making paddles. But I must be patient as they have more than once threatened to leave us.

At 1/4 past 8 got into our canoes, two more difficult rapids passed us and we came into good water, for the greater part dead, permitting us to use paddles. At 1/2 past 9 a.m. reached the first lake, a small pond affair but glad to leave the roaring and troublesome river, a narrow passage of dead water. About 12 m. we reached the beginning of the first great lake about six miles from the entrance of the first. The canoe with the men being far behind, I stopped on the left side to light a fire, cook, and repair my canoe which leaks very much. The direction and course from the entrance of the first lake is S. 80x E. Some lofty hills lie further to the East, various ridges or fragments of them lie in the distance, and one to the right of the 1st big lake, running S.E.-N.W. It may however be the continuation of an axis from the mouth of Madawaska running N.E. up here, which I am inclined to think it is, and that the lakes are formed in this country by the depressed intervals which separate the peaks. All the lakes of this region, including the Temiscouata, Rimouski's sources, those of the [Kedgwick], and the Matapedia, all seem to belong to this category.

At 12 m. the glorious sun, which has never shone upon us since last Sunday, broke out nobly and cheered us very much. At 1/2 past one p.m. continued our journey, the wind being westerly my umbrella assisted us a little as a sail. At the foot of the lake the inlet runs close to the shore and is concealed by rushes. After going about a mile, found it jammed up in various places, obliging us to cut our way through and in some places to lift the canoe over large fallen trees. This lasted about half a mile when reached the third or last lake; at its mouth a beautiful small long fish, weighing about 1/2 a pound with a small mouth and head and silvery scales, was so plentiful in the water that the men killed several with the edges of their paddles. I never saw more fish herding together. It being late we crossed over to a point on the S. side of the lake and encamped upon a dry hill. Having got our establishment in order, we supped and laid down amidst the cry of the solitary owl.

Monday, November 4th. A fine mild morning and the sun out. Glad to leave my bed where I found little comfort. Divided the bread with the Indians, finding they ate twice as much as ourselves. They seemed satisfied with the explanation I gave them. A little after 8 a.m. got into our canoes and proceeded up the 3rd lake about seven miles long to the inlet. The breadth in no part exceeds 1 1/2 miles. By the aid of two paddles and my umbrella spread to a favouring breeze, reached the South end in an hour and a half, where to my great disappointment found the ice had formed entirely over the South end for near half a mile, half an inch thick, covering the channel and rendering it impossible to reach the inlet without stopping at least three hours to break our way. I perceived at once that the back-water of the lake made dead water perhaps for four or five miles up the inlet and that our further progress was stopped. My son was of the same opinion, and as it was freezing very hard, the most important point now was to secure our retreat. I therefore landed on the West side and took the elevation by barometer, which appeared to give about 276 feet above the sea, to which add 15 feet for the source of the lake about 12 miles to the south, and we have 290 feet elevation for the sources of the Mitis, which the people of Maine have not scrupled to impose upon the world for 3,000 feet.

Having thus closed my object in this part of the country, we turned our faces northwards and paddled with all our force against the wind, the waves being tolerably high and the day excessively cold. I paddled for about 3 hours to relieve the little Indian boy and to keep myself warm. In order to accomplish my intention of leaving all the still water behind us, I did not stop to dine today. We found the ice already formed since yesterday half way across the narrowest part of the 1st big lake, and have narrowly escaped being shut in. We reached the mouth of the first and smallest lake a few minutes past 4 p.m. and immediately chose our camp and got our arrangements made as quick as possible to give the men an opportunity to sheathe their canoes with cedar for the descent of the rapids tomorrow.

Tuesday, November 5th. A very cold uncomfortable night. After a miserable night preferred a little before going to sit by the fire, the ground being so hard as to make my bones more than ache. After daybreak got washed and breakfasted as soon as practicable. The Indians occupied making sheaths of cedar, very slow at their work and very provoking. Report made to me that there is water ahead of us, frozen across, through which we shall have to break. How fortunate we have been in turning back in season, and how much fatigue and distress we have been saved by not having to return afoot through ice and snow and without provisions.

At 3/4 past 11 a.m. got into our canoes, when upon advancing were detained some time breaking the ice about an inch thick which had formed across the river. Proceeding on we shot down the rapids with great velocity and made the two first portages before 2 p.m. Stopped at the N. end of the long one, waiting for our canoes, and lit a fire to dry my feet. Travelling on this stream is like being [between] two walls about 30 feet apart, the trees are alike, spruce & birch, and nothing can be more tame and insipid. Passed the 3rd portage when the bands of the slips of Le Mercier's canoe breaking, in which were the servants. I pushed on without stopping to dine, the rapids being very dangerous in some places to shoot, and upon one occasion we were very near broaching to and going over. At 5 reached the place where on our 3rd day's ascent we hung up our beef, and it getting dark, seeing nothing of the other canoe, we stopped for the night. Here we found no good camping place, and but for the exertions of Noël the Indian who was with me, we should have fared miserably this night. He knocked us up a wigwam of eight poles and covering it with bark & branches, and making a fire in front, here my son and myself passed the night, having not a blanket to cover ourselves with, our bed clothes being in the other canoe, together with all our provisions except a little bread. Having the frying pan, my son cooked a little beef and with the aid of the bread we got some supper. The cold night passed tediously. Once or twice I got a nap, but our only amusement was watching and feeding the fire. My mind was occupied thinking of the difficulties we had escaped, and anticipating others to be accompanied by the hard frost.

Wednesday, November 6th. At the first dawn of day got up to eat a morsel, and getting into the canoe started downstream. Pushing on with all our power, and obliged to stop every hour to bail her, we arrived about 1/2 past 1 p.m. within 3 miles of Le Mercier's settlement and found the river blocked up 200 yards with loose ice 8 inches through. Here, wet through, sitting 3 inches deep in the water, our bread all in a paste, and everything ragged and draggled we made a portage through the woods to the open water, embarked again at 3 p.m., passed Le Mercier's and paddling on with every effort, came to another place where the river was blocked up. Here we abandoned the canoe, and loading ourselves with the barometer and my letter case (carried by my son), we started for Mr. MacNider's on foot, my thin leather moccasins all torn to pieces and my feet severely punished by the stubs and roots. Walking through the woods with great vigour, and passing the cataract, we made the distance, 5 miles, in an hour and five minutes, reaching MacNider's at a little after dark. Here we were kindly received, washed, dried, and supped, and worn out with fatigue, went to bed. A northeast high wind with snow threatening a storm.

Thursday, November 7th. A very high storm all night, and snow blowing in every direction. Rose at 7 a.m., much refreshed, got some comfortable sleep for the first time in eight nights. After breakfast paid the Indians off. Storm continuing and the northeast wind driving in the sea into the mouth of the river rendered it almost impossible to hope we can get away today, as there are no means of getting the horses to the opposite shore. The curious circumstances occurred of the tide not receding at all, the whole bay remained full of deep water so that it could not be crossed, a circumstance caused by the violence of the gale and which rarely occurs here. I therefore remained patiently at MacNider's, writing and reading. Towards evening the gale abated but continued snowing. Went to bed about 10 p.m.

Friday, November 8th. Mild weather, light snow falling, the tide very low out, so that we can safely cross. Hurried our breakfast. Old MacNider, who is always half drunk and once a day all drunk, last night shut my men out of the house, who were consequently obliged to sleep at another place. Paid him his account and got away at 11 a.m., his young son John having the kindness to get us across the bay, a very difficult part of our journey, through snow & mud. After two or three miles got into three sleighs I had engaged and drove on as fast as we could with some bad horses.

Stopped to warm ourselves half way at Simon Champlain's. His wife, now not more than 42, has brought him 17 children, 16 of whom are alive, the greater part of whom I saw and are fine looking children. At her accouchements she never remains in bed more than two days, never has a nurse, her other children assisting her, and does all the household work besides taking care of the family. Her husband also is an exemplary, industrious man. On the other side of the river there are three women who have borne their husbands 66 children. This certainly is a very healthy country, free from fevers. At 1/2 past 4 p.m. stopped at Mr. Gauvreau's, the postmaster who recd us very kindly. Madame gave us an excellent supper of trout and tea &c, with preserves, and at 9 p.m. went to a clean bed.

Saturday, November 9th. Cloudy morning, rose at 7 a.m. much refreshed. Breakfasted with Mr. & Mrs. Gauvreau, took leave and walked to Capt. Gardner's to bid them goodbye. Another snow storm set in. Crossed the River Rimouski where found two caleches engaged for me. Went on very well to Old Bic, the place where we disembarked from the *Ringdove*. At the entrance of the new road called the Portage, found the snow 15 inches deep and increasing. Having to break the road, my horse who was first became too fatigued, and after many vain attempts to get him on we stopped and engaged a fresh horse and caleche /and/ driving briskly and giving the tired horse the luggage, we reached Celestin River about 1/2 past 6 p.m., where stopped for the night. Got an indifferent supper, but having the luxury of a sitting room and stove to ourselves, did not mind it. This place is half a league short of Trois-Pistoles, and the distance from Rimouski is estimated at 38 miles.

Sunday, November 10th. Up at 8 a.m. and drove before breakfast to L'Isle-Verte, 5 leagues. Stopped at Mad. Bertrand's to breakfast. Saw about 50 carrioles (one-horse sleighs) at the church door. The family at Mass. A servant got us some tea & eggs, and the little children all began to play at cards, biting small pieces from an apple each of them had for stakes, the winner took all the bitten pieces. To complete the whole affair, when I asked what was to pay, they sent to the church to Mad. Bertrand who came home all *endimanchée* to receive half a dollar. I landed at this house last year from the *Saguenay*. About 1/2 past 2 p.m. reached Rivière-du-Loup and drove to Mr. Davidson's who rec^d us. Dined with them, Mrs. D. and a Mr. Mulligan and his wife. Mrs. D. is a sort of yankeefied woman, hardly able to help herself. After passing a pleasant evening enough, retired to rest.

Monday, November 11th. Breakfasted and began the Grand Portage to Temiscouata, a beautiful morning and an excessively dreary ride, but the snow will enable us to do it in one day, which is very fortunate. Stopped at sunset at a miserable hovel called the Post House, full of foot passengers and labourers who were going to pass the night there. Got some stewed hare and potatoes to eat, good enough. Took the elevations by barometer at the sources of the St. Francis, six leagues from the St. Lawrence, at the top of the Grande Fourche, a lofty ridge, and at the top of another ridge called Jean Paradis, said to be the highest of all. This last we took by torch light at 9 p.m. Reached Lake Temiscouata at 11 p.m. Got in at Mrs. Costigan's, took a cup of tea and laid down. Old Peter and Nadeau came to see me, the first rather lively, having drunk a little in his great joy to hear of our arrival.

Tuesday, November 12th. Up at daybreak and had the party called. Breakfasted. Mr. Chapman the Deputy Commissary called to offer his services. Went with him to look at the public barracks which are well built. After settling some troublesome accounts at the store, got away at 1/2 past 9 a.m. The lake in fine order and a fair wind. This lake [Temiscouata] is about 25 miles long and averages about 17 miles broad.[54] The land is elevated about the lake in an irregular

---

54 The actual average width is less than two miles.

manner, the peaks, following chains in the direction of N.E. & S.W., none of the peaks exceeding 400 feet. The one opposite the portage is about 350 feet. This Mr. Bouchette has reported to be 800 feet high. At the S. end of the lake there is a shallow place called the Degelé [Dégelis] which is said never to freeze during the winter. A tow path is cut on the left bank of the Madawaska. This is a fine stream and the paddles are used all the way to the Saint John. The low land is the bottom of an ancient lake, sand & clay, and the difference of level between the Saint John and Lake Temiscouata proves that the River Madawaska once formed part of L. Temiscouata. We suffered a good deal from cold, and stopped at two places to warm. The last was at the Little Falls (about 7 feet) at the junction with the Saint John. We at length reached Martin's ... at 10 p.m., where found Capt. Maclauchlan the warden. Here we supped. I got a bad and dangerous fall from the step on the frozen ground, and did not get to bed until midnight.

Wednesday, November 13th. Rose in the morning very stiff from my fall. I never ran so great a risk before o'f breaking my thigh. Breakfasted and got into our canoes at 9 a.m. Called at Mr. Langevin's the curée, two miles below, an agreeable man. Gave him instructions to tell his parishioners the Madawaskans that the Americans would never be permitted to advance to the North of the Saint John. The banks of the river are settled very thickly for 5 miles below, and tolerably well settled all the way. The banks are formed of blue and green salt with sands, old lacustrine deposits. The country is all of a low lake level except where the ridges are, so that it is evident all the country from the Falls of the Saint John to the portage of Temiscouata (There is not a single rapid the whole way), except the ridges, has been a continuity of Lake Temiscouata. I doubt whether the difference of level is 60 feet now. Reached the Great Falls about 1/2 past 7 p.m., having worked hard with the paddle myself. Got in at Sir John Caldwell's who is in the U.S. Found a great many letters. All my family, I thank God, well. Sat up until one in the morning answering letters.

Thursday, November 14th. Rose at break of day, breakfasted, got all my business transacted, crossed the portage and in my canoe by 1/2 past 9 a.m. The old diluvial banks below. The present waters have covered the falls for the diluvial and lacustrine banks are continued down the river. Reached the Aroostook in 3 1/2 hours (20 miles). Continued on, a rainy day. Passed the River de Chute, and the place called by the settlers Tayqueesahcowic, and which has been called the settlers Goosaquick, the Canadians having first corrupted it to Goosaquit [Guisiguit]. We landed here on our visit in August to Mars Hill. A heavy rain but continued on to Carr's at the Monquart where arrived at 6 p.m. having made 40 miles. I worked 7 hours steadily at the paddle without drawing it. Here we dried ourselves and supped. The other canoes did not reach us this night.

Friday, November 15th. Up early. Parsons & McQueen joined us about 8 a.m. Found Parsons had given my keys to McGregor,[55] an indiscretion for which I have

---

55 Lance-Corporal William McGregor, an experienced observer, had remained throughout the survey at the Grand Falls observatory where he recorded barometric readings three times daily, to permit a comparison with the field barometers for the determination of height differences.

been for the first time really angry with him. His great fault is want of reflection. With the intention of having the contents of my trunks aired, he gives the keys to a drunken fellow, and despatches and private papers.

Left Carr's at 9 a.m. Took the paddle vigorously. At 1/2 past 3 p.m. passed Woodstock, and at 1/2 past 5 stopped at Jones's, opposite Eel River. Supped indifferently, and having dried ourselves (having rained all the evening), went to bed, pouring torrents of rain.

Saturday, November 16th. Up at 6 a.m. and hurried the people with breakfast. Clear sky and fair wind.

PART TWO

MUDGE'S JOURNAL

24 September to 22 October 1839

Tuesday, September 24th. Still water at the head of the stream running into the lake at the head of the Manasagan [Munsungan] River.

Our voyage was commenced from Fredericton on the 24th of August, in a horse boat, in company with Mr. Featherstonhaugh and his son. The boat was drawn by two horses, one ridden by a mulatto, who seemed indifferent to danger and depth of water, as well as seasoned against cold. One boat was provided with a covered tent in the middle, and was comfortable enough. Our instruments were carefully suspended in it by hooks and nails.

The first day, as we started late, we got but a few miles. The first ferry occurred in the Saint John, from whence we walked to a public house about a mile distant, where we got a tolerable supper. The next morning, starting at six, we got about 20 miles to another public house where we slept, and started again the next morning.

The third day we reached Woodstock, an unpleasant town, full of lumberers, and slept at a house dignified by the name of the Woodstock Hotel, noisy and full of people, all engaged, or interested, in the lumbering trade.

We started the next morning at five, in heavy rain, by a small wagon, holding F. and myself, to the boat 2 miles up the river; and after two more days' voyage, arrived early in the morning of the 30th at a small house near the river, where we breakfasted, and afterwards ascended the neighbouring hill on horseback for about 2 miles, walking the remainder. The ascent was difficult over swamps, and then climbing to the summit, from whence we had an extensive view over the disputed territory. This hill is apparently unconnected with any of the highlands; but Featherstonhaugh is of opinion that it belongs to the ridge extending from the head of the Chaudière River, and forming part of the great chain of the Allegheny Mountains.

We returned to house from whence we started about 4; and after a hearty dinner embarked again, and arrived at a miserable house at the River de Chute after 6 in the evening. Our bedroom was a miserable loft, scarcely watertight, and containing besides ourselves numerous children of the family. Pursuing our journey as usual next morning, we reached the Tobique River, where we hired two wagons, and after crossing the Aroostook River in a horse boat, and stopping for an hour at a small town by the way in the woods, reached the Grand Falls at 6.30 in the evening, the distance, 20 miles, having been performed in 6 and a half hours. Our miserable wagon, in which I drove young Featherstonhaugh, broke down two or three times by the way, and we had great difficulty in reaching the end of our journey.

We were received in the kindest manner by Sir John Caldwell, who has an extensive sawmill at the Falls, and remained with him under his hospitable roof for a fortnight. Featherstonhaugh made his arrangements for our further proceedings; and his expectations of proving the highlands being entirely geological, I have agreed to act entirely according to his views, supposing his knowledge of the geology of America to form the best guide for our further proceeding. He despatched persons from hence for the purpose of procuring the assistance of Canadians, and Indians, and a canoe. I also directed Mr. Wilkinson, the quartermaster of our expedition, to secure me an Indian and a canoe at the Tobique.

The Falls of the Saint John are not so striking as I had expected. The river falls over rocks about 70 feet, and thence downward about 50 feet into a small basin. What interest or grandeur might have attached to the falls has been injured or destroyed by the erection of Sir John's sawmills and railroad. The view is quite confined, and limited to the banks on both sides, which are covered with wood, as are all the summits in this country. The only clearings are on the banks of the river. Sir John's cottage is very small, built entirely of wood, and comfortable enough. My bedroom was under the roof, panelled with wood, as was also the ceiling. During our stay Colonel Ashburnham of the Guards arrived on his way to Quebec; and being unwell, remained two days at the Falls.

Having started our party for the Allagash River, under Mr. Hansard, to form a deposit of provisions there, and to wait our arrival about the 23rd of September, we left the Grand Falls on the 9th, Featherstonhaugh in his canoe with his Indian, young F., with Thomas, in a wagon of the roughest description drawn by two horses, while I rode on horseback, as there was not room for more than two in the wagon. We reached the Tobique ferry at dark. The whole day it rained with great violence, but my coat and trousers were waterproof. We found our party in camp at the mouth of the Aroostok River, and proceeded to the inn opposite to the Tobique, where we slept. An attack having been made on the American Fort Fairfield by a party of lumberers, two nights before, we were apprehensive that our voyage up the river might be interrupted in consequence. Featherstonhaugh therefore rode to the fort on the following day to visit the Commandant; and we were glad to find that a complete discomfiture of the lumberers had put the Commandant in such good humour that he made no objection to our going up the river.

After breakfast on the 10th, young Featherstonhaugh and I walked by the portage road 6 miles to meet our party, to the spot intended for our camp. The weather was hot, and we arrived much fatigued at the river. Unfortunately I missed my footing in crossing a wooden bridge made of a tree, barked on the upper side to form a footing, and fell into the water, wetting myself thoroughly, and worst of all, my chronometer given by the king of Denmark to my father. I had to remain for two hours in my wet clothes till the baggage came from the Saint John River. Happily I did not take cold in consequence, feeling more severely the want of good and wholesome food than anything else, our provisions being slices of very salt pork and biscuit, without bread or vegetables. Our tent, in which we slept for the first time, was comfortable enough, with a good fire in front, and plenty of spruce boughs to lay our beds upon. Our breakfast, like our dinner, consisted of the same fried pork and biscuit; and we remained waiting for Featherstonhaugh till past one o'clock. When he arrived, we went down the river to carry the barometers and other necessary articles to an elevation which he considered belonged to the ridge. This occupied us till 4 o'clock, when we started to proceed up the river.

On an exploring expedition in the morning, I paid a visit to the Commandant at the fort, to whom I had previously sent my card, and was received by him with much civility. His apartment was the upper story of his log house, forming the living and sleeping apartment of himself and several others. I remained half an hour talking on indifferent subjects, and carefully avoiding the boundary question altogether. Shortly before leaving our camp, a young Indian arrived in his canoe for my use. Unfortunately I had left the selection to others, and regretted when too late, that I had not taken the advice of Sir John Harvey to send from Fredericton to secure a good and experienced Indian, as Featherstonhaugh had done for himself. After passing the fort, it began to rain violently, and we arrived at our second camp very wet and uncomfortable. Our tent was erected in the rain, we soon however had a good fire. I was glad to get under it, have some supper, and go to bed.

The next morning we started at 6 without breakfast, to which the men had not been accustomed, and there was much grumbling in consequence. My Indian stopped, and took all my things out of the canoe, refusing to go any further, but after some time he came round, on the promise of a good breakfast and the assurance that another morning he should have his breakfast before starting. The following morning Featherstonhaugh and I went to a neighbouring eminence with the barometers, and returned to breakfast at 8 o'clock. The weather was fine, and during the day I killed three partridges on the trees, near the river, and, on the following day, one. Proceeding in this manner without much interest or variety, we arrived on the 19th instant at the Forks of the Aroostook, where we camped. The river here loses its name, and the two streams which form it are called the Millekenaak [Millinocket] and the Minnesagan [Munsungan]. On the 20th Featherstonhaugh and I started up the former river, he in his canoe, and I in a log one, to trace the river to its source. We took 4 other canoes with us to hold the tent and baggage, and with great difficulty forced them up a rapid and shallow stream to a large lake, forming the head of the river; from whence we had a view of a distant range of hills of some height.

The following morning Featherstonhaugh went on the lake, and I went with a party down the stream to the commencement of a run of still water, where we fished for three or four hours. I caught a great many fine trout and some chub. One trout was about 3 lbs, the finest and most beautiful I ever saw, spotted in the most lovely manner with gold and crimson, scarlet belly and fins, and most beautifully variegated, surpassing anything of the fish tribe I had ever seen. When Featherstonhaugh arrived we proceeded down the river; and at the very first rapid we came to, my canoe was swamped, and we just contrived to get her to the shore without sinking quite, though full of water. All my kit was in her: bed, clothes, bag, fishing tackle; all my spare shoes and boots were full of water, but my clothes and bedding happily escaped, being well wrapped up in my mackintosh hammock, which is invaluable. The injury otherwise sustained was however considerable. We reached the camp in the evening at near six o'clock, instead of performing the voyage as Featherstonhaugh had calculated upon in an hour and a half; I found F. had arrived some time before me. My fish made a capital supper, which with the addition of Irish stew, made of pork, potatoes, and soaked biscuit and butter, enabled us to make a good meal. The Irish stew and soaked biscuit were introduced by myself, and are a very agreeable alteration of the usual fare of fried pork and biscuit.

The next morning, Sunday, we started as usual and arrived at one o'clock at a chain of lakes, three in number, on the shore of the longest of which we dined. During the day we caught several large fish of the trout species, weighing from

2 to 6 lbs and one or two much larger. They are rather dry and inferior to river trout, though very acceptable in our condition, not finding moose, deer or game of any kind, or birds either of any sort, with the exception of a few ducks and crows, which are the sum of all the birds we have seen since we left Fredericton. Featherstonhaugh's Indian Peter has been out looking for moose deer without success, though the traces and footmarks have been very frequent.

Wednesday, September 25th. Yesterday we succeeded only in cutting through a portage of one mile and a half and camped at the end of it. Towards the afternoon two guns were heard and answered; they proved to be the signal of the arrival of Mr. Hansard and his party at the Fourth Lake [Wallagasquigwam or Churchill Lake], about ten miles distant, after ascending the Saint John River and the Allagash to meet us. The signal was fired by Louis, the Indian guide, who had conducted a party of eight men to meet us, leaving Mr. Hansard at the Fourth Lake with the remainder of the men of his party.

Featherstonhaugh is dissatisfied with our progress.

This day we started, F., I and his son, our birch canoes in advance of the party with four other canoes, and our tent and baggage. After cutting through the first portage of half a mile, and passing through some still waters, we came to another small portage, and then to a lake of a mile in length. The wind was high and the navigation unpleasant, but the weather was otherwise fine and dry. After exploring this lake, which did not appear to contain many fish, we came to another portage of two miles and a half, about a half of which we cut through, and camped near the cutting. The method of cutting and passing through these portages, which are all through woods, is to have from four to five axemen in front cutting down the trees and bushes, to make way for the people and canoes to pass. The woods are not only full of timber of the largest size, but are covered also with undergrowth of timber of all sizes, forming a complete obstacle to anything but wild animals.

On our arrival at the termination of this day's labours, we were gratified by the arrival of Mr. Hansard with the intelligence of two moose having been killed on the Fourth Lake by himself and his party. The moose were heard bellowing in the woods, and were surprised late at night, as they were feeding on the margin of the lake. The party fired three shots at the old moose bull, who fell into the lake and in its struggles nearly upset the canoe; the other, a small one, was easily killed, and the cow was wounded but escaped.

The moose are expected to be plentiful; this addition to our stores is very acceptable, as great inroads have been already made into the depot of provisions brought up by Mr. Hansard for the remainder of journey.

After completing as much of the portage as the time of day would allow, we formed our camp as usual, by selecting as dry a spot as could be found, cutting away the trees for room for our tent, and building a large fire in front with the trunks of large trees. The best trees to burn are the maple, birch, and beech. For all encampments the choice depends on the quantity and quality of the timber for fuel. What is called hard wood are best fit for the purpose, while cedars and pines, which are the wood of the country, are not suitable for burning. The bark of the cedar is however invaluable for some purposes; smouldering slowly away when set on fire, it keeps off the black flies most effectually; the frost has however completely dispersed them for the season, or nearly so, but the mosquitoes are still a little troublesome.

After pitching our tent, our dinner or supper was prepared as usual by our servants, of salt pork, soaked biscuit, a few potatoes, which latter are almost expended, and some tea. I slept comfortably during the night, hearing the rain pattering on the roof of our sleeping tent, and within a few inches of my head: but the tent is happily water-proof.

Thursday, September 26th. Rain with a prospect of its continuance. Breakfasted as usual about 7. As for dressing I have not changed since leaving the Saint John, or had an opportunity of drying my clothes, boots and shoes; shaving is out of the question. I have now a beard, growing since we left the Falls on the 9th instant; my razors have been wetted so often that they will hardly perform their office when called upon. My watch I am glad to find goes tolerably, and has not stopped for some days.

Friday, September 27th. Our camp is on the North side of the Fourth or Windy Lake. Yesterday was a terrible day indeed, but by the mercy of God we are none of us the worse for it. We started from our last camp soon after breakfast, the rain pouring down and continuing without intermission during the whole day. We crossed three lakes and five portages, before reaching the South shore of this lake in the evening, the rain blowing from the Northeast, very cold and stormy. I crossed the largest lake in a birch canoe with Mr. Hansard and Louis an Indian, leaving mine to follow; happily we all got over safe. Between this and the Fourth Lake we had portages of a mile and more, to carry the canoes and baggage. We were so wet in landing, that we were forced to build large fires to dry ourselves, a practice in this country indispensable to supply heat, proportionate to that carried off by wet, and cold, and exhaustion.

We reached the last portage about 4, and arrived at our camping ground on the other side of the lake wet and cold, without a change of clothes, or a tent to cover us till long after dark, the bearers of the camp equipage and baggage not having been able to find their way through the woods. We fortunately possessed a lantern which I had brought from London; this we despatched to their aid, and soon afterwards we had the comfort of Queen Victoria over our heads again (Her Majesty's cypher and crown surmount the entrance of our tent), and with a large fire blazing in front we were soon comfortable and warm. Our supper was ready at 8 o'clock, which consisted of five partridges, three I killed, and the other two were knocked down by the men with a stone; they were stewed with a few potatoes, and a little pork, to make an Irish stew, the favourite dish of my invention. As soon as the men had finished their supper, we set to work to make our comfortable beds of spruce branches and mattresses laid on them; most thankful was I to lie down, and I slept soundly till daylight this morning.

The opening of the day had an unpropitious aspect; but a happy termination of the rain enabled me after breakfast to spread out my clothes, baggage, and instruments in the wind and sun to dry, after having been wet and damp for a fortnight, swamped in canoes, tumbled into the river, and dragged in the rain through wet leaves and cedar swamps. Our camp was close to the lake, and we were soon on board, Featherstonhaugh and I in our canoes, Thomas and F's servant following. We crossed the lake, which we had been unable to do yesterday on account of the wind, in half an hour. Shortly after reaching the beach where our depot was placed by Mr. Hansard, we heard a doleful cry from whence we had come; my glass was in a moment to my eye, and I saw that of two canoes containing our servants and the sappers, only one remained on the water. Soon after I perceived two men hanging on to the canoe that still preserved its position; and instantly one of our canoes was pushed off from the beach with men to render assistance; we remained in suspense and alarm for more than half an hour.

When the boats, as they returned, approached near enough for me to distinguish who was in them with my telescope, I was gratified to perceive Thomas and Featherstonhaugh's servant, and the two sappers, and to find afterwards that nothing was lost by the upsetting of the canoe but my fishing rod and umbrella, which are now deposited at the bottom of the lake. Another of our canoes was missing until within the last half hour, and we were apprehensive that the boatman, Michael Curran, one of our best men, was lost. I had long perceived with my glass what I thought to be a canoe with a man in it, on a bend of the lake opposite; and it turned out that I was right, though all the others declared it was only a piece of timber. The poor fellow had been driven by the force of the wind and swell, and was only rescued by our men, when at last perceived by them attempting ineffectually to make his way to the shore. So end our day's disasters.

We are encamped at our depot with plenty of provisions, and waiting for Mr. Wilkinson's party, whom we left the day before yesterday; they will probably not be here till tomorrow at least. We have however sent them provisions, which were nearly all expended when we left them. Featherstonhaugh proposes to discharge a number of men, so as to augment the means of supporting the remainder.

There are plenty of fish in the lake, which are taken with a spear and by angling. Two are this instant brought to me to look at, weighing 8 pounds apiece. What a loss is my fishing rod! But I scarcely regret it, as no loss of life occurred. My umbrella, which I had taken out from the inside of my mosquito tent, and which was a comfort to me many a rainy day, will prove a more serious loss. I am so thankful however, under all circumstances, for unlooked for health and strength, after all the hardship and bad weather I have endured, that I have not a wish to repine at anything.

Saturday, September 28th. A day's rest is a joyous thing after such long fatigue, and without an opportunity of changing anything, or even drying our wet clothes and shoes, which were effectually displayed yesterday to the sun's rays for 3 or 4 hours, while I employed my morning in cleaning my instruments, keeping a watchful eye that the wind did not disperse them over the beach. In the afternoon, we prepared our tent in a very superior manner, the usual covering of birch boughs being laid over the whole, and round the sides, to keep out the wind. Our dinner was served in a much better style, and consisted entirely of hunter's fare. Fish from the lake, boiled, and fried in fat pork, moose meat fried in the same, and a brace of partridges with soaked biscuit for bread, and a couple of potatoes apiece.

We were all in bed by eight. The wind blew very hard during the night, with rain; I rather apprehended that some of our neighbouring tall pines might fall upon us, like those at Beechwood some years ago under similar circumstances; our men however had cut down a good many for firewood. I enjoyed the rest much, listened for some time to the wind and rain, thought of my dear home, and of those who I trust are well there, and recommended us all to the protection of God, with the hope of a happy and early meeting.

This morning we were rather later than usual, breakfasting at eight o'clock. After breakfast I walked to the beach to look after my line, which I set last night, but found nothing on it. On returning, I saw a small fleet of birch canoes on our little beach, which turned out to belong to a party of Indians on a hunting expedition from the Penobscot River, a wild set, but most of them speaking a little English; they had killed one moose two days since and two ducks; they were provided with good guns, and two dogs, one of which I tried ineffectually to purchase. They had been to our tent to give information as to our future route, which appears perfectly satisfactory.

The winter is now evidently approaching, and I look forward to get to the end of the journey with much anticipation of pleasure. This morning on rising, I found the thermometer below freezing point; and a little snow fell for the first time. The air seems to have had full effect on the appetites of our people, who have been stuffing on the heads of the two moose lately killed, stuck on a pole, roasting before the fire, cutting out the favourite bit with their knives, without ceasing, nearly the whole of yesterday and today.

Sunday, September 29th. Yesterday was another delightful day of rest waiting for Mr. Wilkinson and his party, and this day we hope to enjoy another, with the comfort of prayers. Yesterday produced another incident, not less alarming than that of the day preceding. Hearing a moose bellowing on the opposite side of the lake, about a mile distant, Mr. Hansard went over with my Indian, John Michel, in his canoe, wanting me to accompany them, and proceeded with two muskets to shoot the unfortunate cow, supposed to be crying for her calf. I declined going in the canoe, and walked round the shore of the lake to meet them on the opposite side. Going through the wood by the lake, I was tempted to amuse myself with trying to catch a very young squirrel, smaller and more beautiful than the English species; and I had almost frightened the little thing into my hands, when I heard a gun fired. Thinking it was the signal of the death of the unfortunate moose, I waited still to catch the squirrel for nearly half an hour more; then a loud crying and shouting alarmed me, which I still thought announced the death of the animal, and walked to the shore to see what was going on. I put up my glass to my eye, and perceived to my surprise, and alarm, the canoe upset, and the men hanging on to it, at some distance from the shore. My first impulse was to fire both barrels of my gun to encourage them, and alarm the camp, and then to run as fast as I could to procure assistance. The gun brought out several men, and I shouted as loud as possible to tell them what was the matter. Shortly two canoes put off, but with little appearance of arriving in time to do any good. However we soon had the comfort of seeing Mr. Hansard and the Indian arrive at the shore, half dead with cold and exhaustion. The gun I heard fired was the cause of the accident, being overcharged; in firing at some ducks Mr. Hansard overturned the canoe. He could swim, but the Indian could not, and after swimming a little way towards the shore, the Indian cried so much for help that Mr. Hansard returned and encouraged him to hold on, whilst he got on top of the canoe and by slow degrees paddled to the shore, which they reached at last, rejoicing at their happy escape, which indeed was a most narrow one. From the time I heard the gun when the canoe was upset, to seeing them holding on by its bottom, must have been at least half an hour, during the whole of which time, and for half an hour after, they were in the water. A little rum and water hot soon restored them. The Indian complained sadly of Mr. Hansard upsetting the canoe. This has for a time put an end to our canoe shooting; but the Indians went out last night and saw a moose, to which they could not get near enough for a shot.

The night air was very cold, and this morning the thermometer was 29°, we have therefore no expectation of any more fine weather. This morning we had the prayers after breakfast, Featherstonhaugh reading the prayers, and I the responses. No one attended but our servants and the sappers. About one o'clock I descried our party under Mr. Wilkinson approaching from the other side of the lake. They arrived in eleven canoes, an hour after, bringing the rest of our provisions, and some potatoes which we have missed much these last two days.

Monday, September 30th. It rained much yesterday evening, and all night, but today is fine and tolerably mild for the season. We had a little snow on Saturday, but not enough to lie on the ground. The ice has been as much as two inches thick in the morning, after having been drawn in shore during the night. Today our party has been numbered, and twenty men discharged. Featherstonhaugh has determined to go to the north with a small party, with the best men and all the birch canoes. I go down the Allagash River to the Saint John River with another party; then ascend the Saint John to Baker's Lake, where we meet again.

My canoe unfortunately is the worst of the whole lot, unfit for lakes; and my Indian boy again refused to proceed, fearing, as he said, to be upset; threats and promises from Featherstonhaugh, and a little additional coaxing from me, have at last induced him to proceed. The men thought it was unfair. I, however, made no remark and suffered the matter to be so arranged, though certainly the boy had cause for apprehension, as this canoe was the one which was upset two days ago, and nearly drowned Mr. Hansard and my Indian. We left our camp, which has been a home to us for some days, at one o'clock, Featherstonhaugh to the north, and I to the south,[1] with the provisions and discharged men, who are bound for Fredericton and the Great Falls. The day has been uncommonly fine and calm, so that we have passed happily the Windy Lake, which I hope never to see again, in safety and comfort; but I had my swimming belt close at hand, and saw that Thomas had his on. If he had put it on before being upset on Friday, he would have been in comparatively little danger. I am now in my canoe, waiting for the signal to make the portage into the Allagash River.

---

1 Mudge went north, Featherstonhaugh south.

Thursday, October 3rd. After receiving the signal, we began to descend the river, and disembark the heavier baggage, to be carried through the portage by land. We encamped at the end of it. I amused myself with my fishing rod for some time, and in the space of an hour or better I caught a quantity of trout and chub, the former most beautiful fish, especially two of about 2 1/2 lbs each, like those I caught at the end of the lakes on the Aroostook River, scarlet fins and belly, speckled on the body with green, gold and carmine, black mouth and lips as a Blenheim spaniel, and the flesh as red as that of a salmon.[2] The comfort of the quiet which we now have is indescribable; and everything is arranged quietly by Mr. Hansard to my entire satisfaction. The fire placed properly at half the usual distance makes the tent most comfortably warm, and avoids the necessity of our going so close to the fire to get warm, according to Featherstonhaugh's system and practice; thanks to which I have already destroyed both pairs of my waterproof shoes, and a pair of waterproof trousers, so that unless our campaign draws to a close soon, I shall be without clothing to encounter the cold and wet. We passed a most comfortable night, and I enjoyed my breakfast as much next morning.

We started about 9 o'clock, and ascended the River Allagash by several rapids. My Indian boy, who was imprudently selected for me, became alarmed, and was obliged to be removed to another and larger canoe. His place was supplied by an old and experienced Indian, called Bernard, but rendered feeble by age and recent sickness, and unable to sustain much fatigue in crossing the portages. After ascending the rapids, we got into still water, and passed down a succession of lakes. In the first lake we were caught by a storm, but happily we got over in safety with a good deal of tossing though, and a heavy swell. After passing through the chain of lakes, one of which was six miles long, we got again into the River Allagash, a fine broad stream, with a few rapids not dangerous, and landed on the left bank at 3 o'clock. Our supper was as comfortable and nicely arranged as that of yesterday.

No incident of any interest occurred during the day, no game or birds were to be seen, except a baldheaded eagle, at which I fired, of course without effect, and should not have wasted powder and shot, but in the faint hope of getting some quills. The scenery is everywhere similar, and one description might serve for all. Cedars and pines grow to the edge of the water, and nothing is to be seen beyond them, either on the lakes or the rivers. Of course there is no want of good fuel, though the men are careful about that in the selection of a place for camping; they prefer the hard woods, as birch, or beech, to the pines and cedars. It is curious, and would be interesting to our friends at home, to see our preparations for camping. Immediately the word is given, my canoe pushes to the shore, and all the men jump out of their canoes with the greatest alacrity. The ground is so encumbered with growth, that many a noble tree measures its length on the earth in a few minutes, to afford room for our tent, and a fire beyond it. The first thing is a fire, which is soon made with birch bark, sticks and thin trunks of trees; and in half an hour we have fire enough to roast an ox, which is kept continually burning by additional fuel throughout the night.

---

2 Probably a brook trout. Compare Featherstonhaugh's description on the very same day.

I amused myself till dinner time in fishing, and pulled out the chub as fast as my line was put in. One of the Indians took my canoe in the evening, and caught a trout, and a grayling, the first I have seen.

We arrived at the last of the lakes about 12. Beautiful water, gentle, still, and calm. Our party, who were dismissed from the North Lake, were here waiting for us, as desired by a special message sent in advance; and we took from them a canoe to replace one which was injured in the rapids yesterday. We left her alone in the midst of the waters to swim as long as she could; nearly full of water she was then. If I had known what we had to encounter immediately afterwards, I would certainly have taken her on, to see her go alone down the rapid. After crossing the lake, we came to a rapid about half a mile, and then to another stile on the water two miles long. The mode of navigating these rapids is by one or two boatmen standing up and guiding the canoe with their long poles, to prevent it from touching the rocks, which would demolish it in a moment. As soon as the boatmen come near a rapid, they lay aside the paddles, and lay hold of the long poles they have; which are about 20 feet long, and as thick as a man's wrist. We came down these hills in the water in a very fine manner, and the men stopped at the bottom to dine. Here comes another fall, but I am now almost accustomed to it, and see without concern the huge rocks, rising on either side, with the water apparently ready to tumble into the canoe, knowing too that, in case of an upset, it would roll over the occupants to the bottom, if nothing worse came of it.

Saturday, October 5th. We left our camp yesterday after breakfast, the morning was cold with snow and hail. The distance from the camp to the falls was about five miles; at the falls we overtook our party who had encamped there all night. After leaving the falls it began to blow a heavy gale of wind, with some showers and hail; so intensely cold was it, that to write in a canoe was impossible. My corporal [Hearnden], an active able bodied man, complained of being colder than he ever was in his life. Added to this, the wind was north east, directly in our faces, making so much swell that we could not see the rocks; the consequence was we had a perilous time of it, especially as from the falls to the junction of the Allagash and the Saint John River, it was one continued rapid, so bad in some places that the Indians and Frenchmen called out, "*Bien mauvaise cette rapide là.*" This was about a mile long, full of rocks, and breaking water, and the velocity very great. The danger perhaps appeared greater than it really was, though at the bottom we found the party before us had lost one canoe, and upset others, the men belonging to which had made a fire on the bank to dry themselves. Our party were also suffering so much from the cold, that we were obliged to stop for half an hour to get warm by a fire also. After entering the Saint John River, we turned our heads up the stream, and encamped a little inside the woods, near the river about half a mile above the Allagash, on the same side. Our fires were lighted in a few minutes, and we were all comfortably under shelter from the rain and wind in about half an hour. Our dinner consisted of the beautiful trout, and moose meat made into Irish stew.

This morning my Indian, John Michel, was dismissed. We purchased his canoe, in which I am now writing, going up the Saint John with a cold north wind, but the sun shining bright. Last night was cold, the thermometer this morning was at 17° at seven o'clock. The walls of the tent were covered with snow, within a few inches of my head, yet, thank God, I have not yet suffered from the severe work of yesterday, which the Indians pronounced to be the first day of winter. I have made a different arrangement today: sitting with my back to the head of the canoe, the wind having also turned, and with the sun before me, I am enabled to hold a pencil.

[Sunday], October 6th. Yesterday was a charming day, though a cold wind, the sun was shining bright all day. The snow afforded the means of walking the rapid, which I did, along the shore, where it was so warm as to heat me a good deal. I measured the height of the rapid, but it was nothing like that we descended on the Allagash the day before.

We encamped as usual about 5 o'clock; we had a trout for dinner, the fellow to that of yesterday, and one which I caught before dinner, cleaned it myself, and actually put it warm out of the river into the boiling water; it was delicious. This life is not unpleasant; its only drawback is it is the wrong side of the Atlantic, which separates me from those I never wish to leave again.

This morning I rose fresh and hungry, and enjoyed my breakfast of soaked biscuit and moose meat. It froze very sharply in the night, the thermometer when I arose at half past 6 being under 22°. It was cold certainly, but much less than might have been imagined; we had however, it must be confessed, a fire large enough to roast a sheep. After despatching our breakfast, which was over by half past seven, Thomas came running to me with the intelligence that a herd of caribou were on the other side of river. I quickly got rid of the shot in my gun, and put in two balls, and ran down to the side of the river. The caribou had taken alarm, I found, at some stupid Frenchmen, who instead of hiding themselves in the bushes, had crowded down to look at them; the animals however strode away, quietly feeding within 200 yards directly opposite our camp. Before I could get into the canoe to run over to them, they began to move off, and I was obliged to fire twice ineffectually at the bull, after which they started off, but not very fast. The herd consisted of a male, female, and a young one. The bull as big as a two year old heifer, with magnificent antlers, it was marked white on the side.

I wrote this journal in my canoe, with the thermometer 32°, without gloves, and my fingers scarcely cold! My journal has been interrupted by a chase after wild ducks; I longed to have killed two, but the motion of the canoe shakes my hand dreadfully; as it was, I had one, but it saved itself by diving and sliding under the rocks. We stopped to dine just before 12, which gave me an opportunity of taking an observation to ascertain the time, as we have no watch which goes even decently, including my chronometer which stops when exposed to the cold. I am obliged to put it under my head at night. We dined where old Louis encamped on a hunting expedition two years since; his wigwam was still standing, and the old fellow cooked his dinner before me in his former home. The wigwam was constructed by a forked stick in a leaning position, with others resting upon the fork, forming about three-fourths of a circle, with flat layers of birch bark covering all from top to bottom, just as he had lived in it with his squaw two years ago, by no means an uncomfortable dwelling. Louis told me it did not take more than half an hour to make! How easily are our actual wants supplied! I could have slept in the wigwam with comfort, and would much rather do so than in a tent.

We continued as pleasant a party as ever; there is but one Englishman besides myself; amongst the rest are Canadians, and my old Indian. The Canadians are a cheerful set, always singing French songs and laughing, far better company than the blue-noses we have dismissed.

[Monday], October 7th. Although the subsistence of the party, we expect to meet at the lake at the end of this river (Bathurst [Baker] Lake), depends on our meeting them at the earliest possible time, I have not forgotten that this is a day which ought to be kept sacred, and trust that the urgency of the case will justify our proceeding as usual this day. It is a comfort for me, that having lost our lumbering friends, the Irish blue-noses of Fredericton, we are no longer annoyed with their swearing and noise, which continued without the slightest provocation or cessation from morning till night. My Indian, who left us yesterday, was sensible of the disregard paid to the Sabbath; he amused himself and pleased me, by singing a hymn in Indian, which he had learnt at the chapel, all the Mohawks being Catholics in this part of America. An Irishman began to abuse him one day for singing on Sunday; his reply was, "Indian sing song he learn in chapel; Englishman swear, swear, all day Sunday; this no good." This lad was only 18.

We encamped yesterday at the head of a rapid early, to allow the heavy canoes to come up before dark. I ventured, for the first time, to choose the camping place, which was approved of, as the most comfortable place we have met with during all our long journey. It was situated on the left bank of the river, looking down it, about 10 feet above the river on a level bank, covered with wood fit for fuel and bedding. A beautiful clear brook ran close to it from the hills behind and immediately beneath our feet a rising hill in the wood, covered with silver and spruce firs. As soon as the camp was fixed, I took my fishing rod, a very rough piece of work, manufactured to supply the place of the one now at the bottom of the Fourth Lake, and in an hour caught a number of beautiful trout, which came in very well for breakfast next morning; the servants had their share of them. Our Indians are lazy, having plenty to eat. It is a characteristic of the North American Indians to eat as long as anything is left, and only to hunt when hunger presses, or when everything eatable is gone, even to a lump of sugar.

Accordingly, although the river is full of trout, I cannot get anybody to go and catch them, though an hour's fishing by torchlight would probably supply us with enough for some days. I must trust to my own rod, I believe, for so acceptable an addition to our dinner. Yesterday we opened a case of haricots, but which we found to be indifferent French beans, and a case of ox-tail soup, pretty good, which we deal out a spoonful at a time, to put into the Irish stew.

My scientific journal contains all matters of a scientific nature, not included here, but I cannot refrain from remarking that, from my own observation, I am more than ever convinced that my friend Featherstonhaugh's theory will never settle the question. Louis and I get on very well together jabbering French; he speaks English a little, but prefers French. In talking to me, some of the Frenchmen speak a little English, but I have to act as general interpreter; as Mr. Hansard, to whom I commit the entire management of the expedition, does not speak French. This day has been indifferent, but on the whole we have nothing to complain of, and everything to be thankful for. Good health beyond my most sanguine expectations, and plenty of good food, which I suspect however, may become scarce before we reach Quebec, so that I consider it necessary to fish as much as possible to save our moose, pork, and biscuit. If I had brought down the bull caribou yesterday, we should have had a fine feast and abundance. But we are in a fine hunting country, and approaching a better both for moose meat and fish.

I have had some pleasant exercise today in walking up the rapids, it rained a little at times but not much, a little however, is nearly as bad as a good deal, on account of the long grass and trees by the side of the river, through which we have to pass. This part of the country is all under water in the spring; and the roads, such as they are, are then close to the river's edge, and I expect it would be a matter of great difficulty to get through them, as trees upon trees lie in every direction one upon another, which have fallen unnoted from the earliest ages. The cedar forms the great majority of these; it is a wood which takes many years to rot; it may be called the wood of the country. The Indians use it much to make canoes, the one I am now writing in is made of it, except the outside covering which is of birch bark.

Tuesday, October 8th. By a mistake in our reckoning, very possible in our present mode of life, I made yesterday Sunday, instead of the day before; but I shall keep my almanack now always at hand, and shall guard against a similar error in future. We proceeded, as usual, yesterday till five, when we camped in a pleasant spot in the woods near the river, but no beautiful brook to supply us with delicious cold water. The river water is not unwholesome, but it has a flavour. Our dinner, as usual, of beautiful trout, and a hotch potch of pork, potatoes and part of the contents of a can of mock turtle; but we voted my old mixture, the Irish stew, more simple and preferable. The trout are certainly a great luxury, and far finer flavoured than any I have ever met with in Europe, except in Loch Leven, where they are as good. When caught I give them a blow on the head, saw them immediately into three or four pieces, afterwards clean them, and hang them on a forked stick, ready for cooking.

We have not seen any caribou or game of any kind, yesterday or today; but moose abound, as is evident, on the banks of the river and by the sides of the rapids.

We stopped for the men to dine, and to get the latitude, at half past one. Notice was given of partridges drumming in the woods, and I went with Louis to look for them, but without success. The drumming of the partridges is the noise made by the cock, who sits on a stone or the branch of a tree, something like the faint tapping of a muffled drum; he does it most probably to give warning to the brood of danger. The Canadians and the Indians consider the drumming of the partridges to be the prelude of a fine autumn. This country seems to be an exception to the general character of North America, as regards the animal creation. The aquatic and other migratory birds, which periodically visit all the rest of the continent in vast numbers, appear to avoid this district, either because it is out of the track towards their southern destination, or from the unfavourable nature of the climate. I do not believe we have seen 20 pigeons altogether, and above half as many ducks. No rabbits we have met with, and but a few hares, which are white in the winter. There are a few squirrels also, which are shot, as well as the rats, for food. These rats are of a large species, as large nearly as a cat, which frequent the banks of the rivers and are distinguished from the common rat, not only by their size, but by the form of the tail, which is vertically flattened, like that of a beaver, but not so broad. The rats build themselves houses in the water, much in the same manner as the beaver, where rushes abound, as large (and not unlike also in appearance) as a large potato cave in Devonshire. Twenty or thirty are sometimes killed by the Indians in one of these houses. Almost the only bird which frequently disturbs the stillness of the woods, is the large woodpecker, whose tap sounds like the blow of a large hammer. Whilst in the woods looking for the partridges, I observed frequent tracks of the moose and bear; the latter is very fond of the bark of the spruce fir, and from the number of trees barked it would appear to be a very favourite food.

Our little fleet of canoes goes merrily up the river, all in good humour, good spirits, and good health. Some of the boats are heavily laden still, with barrels of pork and biscuit to last us during the remainder of the expedition. My canoe is the only one not laden with provisions, being the only birch one; I carry in it only my bag and bundle of clothes; my bag holds little more than a pair of shoes and the remnants of my burnt boots, which Thomas is now converting into a case for a hunting knife, to hang at my side, like Louis the Indian, and which I need much for many purposes, particularly for preparing my fish dinners. My bundle, containing all my clothes and a few silk handkerchiefs, is enclosed in a macintosh hammock, and covered with an oilcloth; my bedding is in another canoe, and consists of a buffalo skin, hair mattress, and blankets. Besides this my canoe contains my fishing rod, of native manufacture, my gun by my side in an india-rubber case, and a barometer fastened to the front of the canoe, that it may not be lost like the former by an upset. I sit with my face to the head, and Louis stands up behind me with a long pole, pushing it forward up the river, and paddling in still water, sitting down. Louis' figure is very good, with an old red nightcap on his head, his long black locks hanging below it, and a sort of Indian frock with leggings, made of deerskin; his costume and his marked expression of countenance, and skin of darkest yellow brown, give him a picturesque and striking appearance. All his baggage is likewise in the canoe; it consists of a small iron pot for cooking, a little flask for holding gum for mending the canoe, and a blue bundle containing gunpowder, balls, tobacco, charms, in short the whole of his campaigning kit. I sit in considerable comfort at the bottom of the canoe, with thin planks spread under me on the bottom, then spruce boughs, then a tarpaulin, and on the top a cushion; pretty well taken care of, it might be said, yet I have had the water over all, more than once. It is a curious sensation going up hills in the water, though not such nervous work as going down. Pushing up against the hill, passing the huge rocks, which you may often touch with one finger, and which I have often done, to keep the canoe off, is startling enough; and though writing with considerable ease and security, I am often reminded that I am not in a mail coach in England. The most difficult thing to maintain in canoeing is balance, to keep exactly in the centre, and happen what may, never to lay hold of the sides, which would infallibly upset it. I am as knowing as an Indian now in finding out a good camping place. The first thing is the choice of a place with plenty of wood, birch, maple and beech, the next to select a level spot, shelter from the winds and near the river, and the last to have a brook or a spring near; which, though not so needful as the other requisites, is a pleasing luxury. With attention paid to these particulars, one is free from cold even in severe weather. Last night the tent was too warm, and this morning I sat at breakfast without my coat at 8 o'clock. Thomas has made an admirable job of my burnt boots; the hole is capitally cobbled up with a piece of the other.

Nothing but rapids - up, up, up all day long; but tomorrow I am comforted with the promise of "*l'eau morte*", which means still water.

Wednesday, October 9th. We stopped as usual at five o'clock; our camping ground is a tolerable place, but there is no spring water. The afternoon and night were very warm, the thermometer 58°, 30 degrees higher than it was three days ago. Breakfasted again with our coats off, on soaked biscuit and moose meat. The old bull moose, which was killed at the Fourth Lake, is now brought into consumption for the first time; as the calf of which we have hitherto eaten is nearly expended. The steak of the bull is like very coarse beef, that of the calf somewhat like veal, but both have a decided flavour.

This morning we started about nine o'clock, and soon after arrived at an open expanse of the river, containing eight large islands. This is a favourite hunting ground of the Indians; and the fresh marks of moose and other wild animals, were all along the banks. We found a party of Indians hunting amongst these islands, the same we met on the Fourth Lake. They had just caught a beaver, which we found scarcely dead in the canoe, and quite warm. I purchased the tail to take home, and also the tail of a musquash. The bargain was made with a little maple sugar, and some gunpowder, with one of my flasks.

Our Indian friends are again come up to us hunting for a beaver trap. One, lost when last we met, has since been found with a beaver in it. I am trying through my interpreter Louis to get a bit of the animal for dinner; but it seems that they have left it on shore as they came up, or we might have had some. While writing I am watching them hunting in the long grass and rushes by the side of the river for the unfortunate beaver and trap. This is an incident which may not occur again in the journal of a European in these parts of North America. The distance of the beaver lakes from the settlements is so great that few persons are likely to undertake the journey; and the animal is also nearly exterminated, and will be entirely so before long, owing to the avidity with which it is pursued by the Indians, who do little besides hunting, not even taking the trouble to fish, although great quantities of fish might be taken in any of the rivers. In all the rivers of this country there is not a single net, except at one or two places on the Saint John and the Aroostook.

The tribes are diminishing rapidly without apparent reason; those at least of this part of the country are evidently well off, always able to maintain themselves, and universally trusted by the whites. My Indian has five children, an unusual number.

No rapids today up to half past eleven, when we stopped for the men to dine, while I spent my time in catching a fine dish of trout for supper. My hunting knife came into great requisition for cleaning the fish. It would also serve to put an end to a poor moose, if we were to meet with one, and I should be glad to take a pair of horns home, of my own killing, they are great weight and size.

Thursday, October 10th. We camped last night about half way up a long rapid, at least two miles long; no incident occurred beyond the usual routine.

Friday, October 11th. The journey yesterday produced nothing interesting, except that we did not catch any trout and felt the loss of them at dinner. In the morning Louis pointed out a spot in the woods near the river, where a couple of years since he buried two of his children, who died of the smallpox. The weather cleared up in the afternoon and the sun shone out, but there was a cold wind, and this morning the thermometer was down again to 22° at 7 o'clock.

We arrived at the forks of the Saint John, where the river divides into two branches, at 9 o'clock. The Southwest branch leads directly to Quebec, a two days journey by portage and canoe. We are now penetrating the interior by the other branch, in order to reach the source of the Chaudière.

Louis has just called out to the Canadian boatmen, "*Si on veut manger de l'orignal (moose) il ne faut pas chanter pour le jour,*" so on we push. The wind is so cold, though the sun shines, that I can write no longer, and must put on my gloves. Our canoe leaks most abominably from the numerous thumps the fragile surface of the bark has sustained, against the sharp rocks. I have delighted my Indian, by producing my large sponge, which at this season, alas indeed at any season in these parts, is of no use; for its original purpose of cold water sponging from head to foot, is not practicable in the woods during the summer on account of the mosquitoes and flies, which would soon make one blister from head to foot, and in the autumn and winter, the cold renders it out of the question; my sponge is therefore applied to emptying the canoe to Louis' great delight, who never saw such a thing in his life before.

I hear the partridges drumming again. What a bore it is to be without a dog; this comes of trusting to others. Instead of an old experienced Indian, and an active young dog, I found myself with an old dog half blind, and quite deaf, which was useless and soon lost, and a young boy of eighteen. I had plenty of exercise yesterday by walking along the shore. If it was not for the numerous moose, it would be extremely difficult to make one's way. These animals have cleared a path everywhere through the bushes and long grass; and the tracks and foot marks by the side of the river on the sand are like those of so many oxen constantly passing and repassing.

Saturday, October 12th. Here I am, thank God, in my canoe again, a result I had much reason to doubt two hours ago. We camped as usual last night, our progress during the day having been much impeded by bad rapids, which obliged us to walk through the woods, and the men to carry the canoes up the stream by going into the water. This morning we started early, anxious to reach the lake about five miles before us. I walked for some time, guided by Mr. Hansard, who having been accustomed to the business of exploring, I considered was a safe pioneer. After a time I fancied that we seemed to be going away from the river, and accordingly insisted on gaining the bank to ascertain the position of our party, who are always making noise enough to be heard a mile off. When we arrived at the river, we saw or heard nothing of them; I fired off my gun several times, and then we became alarmed, and uncertain whether we had not fallen on the course of some tributary stream, the least of the consequences of which would have been perhaps a night or two in the woods, without food or shelter; and I confess, I never was more seriously alarmed. In this dilemma I asked Mr. Hansard if there was no way of ascertaining by signs on the stream or rocks, whether the party had gone up or not. He shook his head, and I agreed to remain on the spot with my corporal, [Hearnden], a capital fellow, whilst Hansard should return on our steps to where the party was last seen, and trace the river upwards, to ascertain whether we were on the right river or not. After he left us, I tried to light a cigar, to pass away the time till his return, with a piece of bark taken from a birch tree, not to use one of the five matches I had left, which might be needed for lighting a solitary fire at night. It then occurred to me, that as the river was remarkably still, without any ripple or current, that in passing up, if the canoes were before us, the agitation of the water must have wetted the rocks far above the water mark. On examination I found this to be the case; and the discovery, which I communicated to my companions, was a great relief to us, as we were now certain that the canoes were before us on the same river. Again I fired off my gun twice, and we all shouted as long and as loud as we could.

In about half an hour, we thought we heard a shout coming down the stream, and to that answered by another gun and shouting; we soon became certain that we were heard, and shortly after one of the men joined us with the information that the rest of the party were about a mile ahead. I despatched him after Mr. Hansard, and waited on the spot for the return of Hansard, who came back to us in about half an hour afterwards, without ascertaining further than that we were on the right stream. No one, who has never been under similar circumstances, can ever estimate the extent of mental distress we endured at the thought of being lost in a wilderness with the prospect of ultimate starvation. But thanks to God, who has preserved us hitherto, we overtook the party soon after, who received a severe rebuke for leaving us, though perhaps we only were in fault for losing sight of the river.

Sunday, October 13th. Sunday again in the canoe, where today I must offer up my prayers, heartily, as I trust, thanking God for his past mercies, and praying for a continuance of them, and blessings on those I so dearly love at home.

Yesterday our progress was so much impeded by the rapids, that we made but little way, and are now at least three miles from the lake, with a very bad rapid of a mile and a half before us. Yesterday I killed a beautiful partridge, nearly as large as a pheasant, different from any I have ever seen. The back was like that of the Azores partridge, and altogether with the exception of the eyes very similar in appearance to it. The legs feathered like a grouse, with two black plumes on each side of the head. I mean to have it stuffed when we get to Quebec.

In the afternoon we observed a stick, stuck up on the side of the river, with a piece of burnt bark folded, and black on the inside. On examination I made out an Indian inscription, well written and perfectly legible, purporting that, André Thomas, an Indian chief, had there killed a moose, whose remains and bones we found lying on a frame and dried. Shortly afterwards a boat, which had advanced in front of mine, made a sign to approach, as the men had seen two moose just before the head of the boat; my gun, in which I keep neither shot or balls, both of which are kept in my waistcoat pocket, was ready with balls in both barrels in a moment, but Louis not being quite so quick, detained us for a minute or two, which gave them time to go off; this they did very quietly however, staring some time at the Indians.

They were both cows, in fact the banks of the river are trodden by them, like cows in a farm yard, and if the Frenchmen can be made to hold their tongues, we cannot fail to get one. This morning Hansard whilst washing by the side of the river before breakfast, heard one lowing very near; Louis went after it, but unsuccessfully. We have already passed the carcases of three, hung up by the Indians, since we left camp this morning. I had a great inclination to take the skins, but property in these wild regions is more respected by the Indians, than by us whites.

Monday, October 14th. We toiled all yesterday till near one o'clock pulling the canoes up the rapids by main force, my canoe being almost torn to pieces; we despaired almost of ever reaching the lake. About two or half past a party was descried on the river, which proved to be a party of Indians with Featherstonhaugh and his party. The Indians had killed a large moose the day before, and Featherstonhaugh's Indian one also, left about three miles off. This occurred very fortunately, and relieved them from the apprehension of being without food, they having nearly expended all their stock.

This journey had taken them the same time to perform forty miles, that had taken us two hundred. In coming up the rapids this morning, in as short a time as possible with provisions for the maintenance of our new party, my canoe got so much injured that it would not swim; and my Indian was obliged to search for gum to patch it up. The consequence was that the party had two or three hours start of me; happily I detained the canoes containing my tent and provisions, and I had reason afterwards to rejoice at my determination to do so, for when the canoe was mended, it began in half an hour to leak again, and was completely swamped, so that Louis had to return to his patching. Featherstonhaugh is now four hours ahead, and we may not overtake him till he reaches the lakes, where we meet to go to Quebec. The Indian hunters left us this morning and returned again this afternoon; they overtook us as we came down the river bringing with them a fine pair of moose horns and head, which I intend to present to the Natural History Society of Plymouth.

By a curious coincidence our camp is pitched on the very spot where we were lost on Saturday; if Featherstonhaugh had carried off my tent and provisions, we should have had to camp on this spot with nothing but the sky over us.

Tuesday, October 15th. The damaged state of my canoe which obliged us to leave the carcase of a moose at the head of one of the rapids, prevented our moving today till near one o'clock. We were obliged to engage our Indian friends, who camped with us last night, to assist in putting on a sheathing to the birch canoes. We dined in comfort last night, with our usual allowance of trout caught by me, in about an hour, whilst the men stopped to get the canoes patched, and delicious moose meat, of the best flavour, and tender as a chicken. Our Indian friends supplied us with some game, amongst them six wild ducks very large and fine, (a drake and a duck of a rare species I intend for the Natural History Museum at Plymouth), in return I gave them a pound of gunpowder and some shot, for which they said, "Thank you", a very unusual thing for an Indian, who usually gives and receives without the least sign or expression of emotion or pleasure. This indifference, which is real and not affected, is the most striking mark in their character. A friend told me he went to a wigwam with a hunter after a long absence to witness his meeting with his family. He scarcely noticed his squaw; and the only notice she took of him was to cook sufficient meat for the food of both.

We are now supplied with abundance of provisions, so that I would not kill a poor moose if it were to cross my path, which is very probable. The dogs have just put up some partridges, which are settling on the trees close to me; but I have no pleasure in killing, when we do not want for food, though I have a loaded gun by my side, and ammunition in abundance.

We are now out of the rapids; for about six miles we have been going steadily down the stream; warm as summer it is, yet tomorrow may bring ice, so uncertain and variable is the climate. This is the only time of the year when the woods are endurable, the flies in the warm weather destroy all comfort. Cedar bark is the only protection.

In the fly season those who enter the woods carry a small switch, smouldering away like a slow match, giving a good deal of smoke and a most agreeable aromatic odour, which the flies cannot bear.

I am now looking forward to reach Quebec in about a week, trusting that the most difficult part of our arduous undertaking is at an end, and perfectly satisfied that the British claim is founded upon truth and justice, but equally certain that the Americans will never allow it. In fact the present generation of Americans have been led by their parents to think their cause a good one; and such impressions are not likely to be erased by the most indisputable arguments. A compromise is all that can be effected without going to war, which would be ruinous to all, and more especially to the people of New Brunswick, who would soon be overrun by swarms of vagabonds from all parts of the States, if even they were capable of coping with the population of Maine, the hardiest and best set of people in America.

Wednesday, October 16th. Yesterday shortly after three we overtook Featherstonhaugh and his party; and are now encamped at the forks of the river, preparing to ascend the river Dougnen [Daaquam], being the nearest road to Quebec.

Praise and thanks to God, that he has given me health and strength to arrive thus far, and to have succeeded in almost completing our expedition, which the most healthy and robust might occasionally have looked at with apprehension, not so much from personal fear on the score of health or strength, but from the certainty that a failure in either must interrupt and impede the operations in which I have been engaged. I have had a most satisfactory conversation with Featherstonhaugh, and we are quite agreed as to the mode of proceeding, and of our report, which has given me more pleasure than anything else. He is so heartily tired of the expedition, that he declares no temptations of any kind shall induce him to undertake another; and if I can reasonably and honourably get off I shall feel the same way. Not that any future expedition would be attended with one half the hardship and expense that this has been. We have arranged that I go from Quebec to New York and meet him there on November 20th; he returns first of all to Fredericton to settle some affairs. I propose to remain a day or two at Quebec to rest and go to Church, and then to proceed to Montreal and Niagara.

We are now proceeding up the River [Daaquam], I in my canoe as usual; some of the party are walking by the portage to meet the canoes at a fork, about five miles up. I have had much praise from my Indian Louis, for finding by the marks of the water on the rocks that the canoes had passed up when we were lost the other day. This morning it threatened to rain, but it cleared off and the fine weather continues. The river is tolerably free from rocks and shoals.

We stopped for the men's dinner at a point terminating a portage, it was the site of an Indian camp, the walls on two sides of which were left standing and complete. It is the most complete thing that could be imagined or contrived, composed of upright stakes driven into the ground, with rafters on them, tied with cedar thongs stripped from the bark, and covered, front, top and sides with bark from the spruce fir, tied on neatly and firmly with cedar thongs. The whole had a symmetrical and comfortable appearance. The doorway was cut in a semi-circular form. These wigwams were 12 feet long, by 10 feet wide, and about 7 feet high in the middle, with a hole in the top to let out the smoke. The fire is placed in the centre, and a door at each end. A sort of railwork was arranged in the roof over the fire, of sticks, and skins placed there to dry; many of which still remained, as those of the muskrat and the moose; there were remains also of a deer and a moose, long strips of the flesh of each being hung up to the roof; in this way the Indians cure by smoke only, without salt, moose and other meat which will keep a year or more. Two rough canoes also remained, one made of the light branches of cedar, covered with bark, and tied together with thongs, and the other hollowed out from the trunk of a large tree, both apparently made for mere secondary purposes to cross the river; from which it appears, according to Louis' inference, that these Indians came without canoes of their own, and made them somewhere up the river, and that they came down the river in these canoes, and afterwards when they left the spot started on their journey by land. There were some wooden stools in the building, and numerous contrivances for drying various skins of value, such as beaver and others, which showed that the hunt had been successful, and a small sieve which, notwithstanding the prohibition, I took the liberty of carrying away as a relic of the camp.

The prohibition alluded to was written on a tree near, on a large piece of bark sliced off for the purpose; the crown above was well drawn, and the letters remarkably well formed, the matter used in writing was apparently red chalk. Here are two interesting proofs of a considerable advance of education amongst the Indians. The language has the appearance of some identity with that of the South Sea Islanders. It appears from Louis' account that the Indians were first taught to write by the French, and that subsequently this most useful acquirement has been carefully transmitted, amongst some of the tribes, from father to son. The Indians of this country are certainly a most respectable class, honest, always holding property in the utmost respect; the mere claim, as the inscription shows, being a sufficient security except from white thieves, such as myself; I believe, however, that my character stands sufficiently high amongst them, to make me welcome to what I may take away. A very remarkable instance of Indian honesty occurred the other day. One of our Indian hunters, André Thomas, the same who wrote and left the inscription over the remains of the moose, which we found when ascending the lakes last week, and who has subsequently been employed by us, had killed in a short time six fine ducks, which I purchased from him for about four shillings. During the negotiation he caught sight of a telescope which belonged to Hansard, of superior make, and was anxious to purchase it at any price; but I explained to him, as he very well knew, that it was one of the most useful articles we had. On leaving the camp next morning Hansard left it behind, and did not miss it till the evening, when André Thomas brought it to him. André had remained in the camp after we had left, and found what he most coveted. I did not know this till afterwards, or he should have had at least another pound of gunpowder, which next to the telescope would have pleased him most.

Old Louis will make quite a fortune by his journey with us; already he has amassed riches in abundance, empty bottles, jars full of oil, pots and pans, all of which he has placed in a cache by the side of the river, like our dog Pucksey hiding a bone! I intend to send him a present of blankets with some other little things, from Quebec.

Although the weather is so fine, the Indians were right, that the cold we had so severely a fortnight ago, was the first day of winter. It has frozen more or less every night since; and almost all the leaves are gone from the trees, the first change after this Indian summer, as it is termed, and ice and snow will soon be in abundance. Moose tracks still continue as frequent as ever, with those of the deer and the bear. Yesterday I am sure there was a bear concealed on an island, where I was, from the tracks and the freshness of the peeling of the bark from the trees. I did not have my gun in my hand, and did not care to examine the cover too closely. A man with presence of mind, and a knife, may almost always kill a bear, by suffering the animal to take him into his paws without struggling. It is their habit to convey off their prey to their haunt without injury, except in case of resistance. The young Indians are taught never to struggle in such cases, if a bear should surprise them, which is not an uncommon occurrence, but to use the knife, which they always carry about in a sheath by their side, firmly and vigorously on the first favourable moment, against the soft part of the belly, cutting up to the heart; they are also frequently killed by the tomahawk.

I could have caught any quantity of trout today, if I had had proper tackle; all my hooks are gone, except for some small ones, which would not hold the fish. I am only surprised that this country has never been visited by Englishmen — a party from Quebec or Fredericton, with their canoes, three officers for instance — with two servants, one for cooking and another to look after the camping;

provisions for two months, three Indians for the three birch canoes, and two Canadians for the two log ones. In about a fortnight such a party might reach the hunting grounds on the Allagash or the Saint John, where they could subsist entirely on game and fish. Any number of trout might be taken with the spear, used for the purpose in these parts; it is made of two pieces of wood, tied together so as to form a spring, and opening to admit the fish, and having a spike in the middle which goes through the back and gills of it immediately. The spear handle is usually about ten or twelve feet long. This is a much better contrivance than anything we have in England. The size of the spear is regulated by the size of the fish intended to be taken, so that the body of the fish should be enclosed in the opening and tightly compressed.

We have again met with another production of André Thomas; three canoeing poles were left standing up, by the side of the river, with a birch bark letter stuck on a cleft stick as before, intimating that they were to be left alone. I am afraid our people have not respected his injunctions this time.

Tuesday, October 22nd. This journey concluded, as regards our voyage by boats. We proceeded up the river to its source nearly, and then twelve miles through the woods to the Lake Etchemin, which was fifty miles from Quebec; from thence we walked a greater part of the way, and arrived here safe and well, through God's protecting Providence, yesterday at two o'clock.

EPILOGUE

After leaving Featherstonhaugh at Quebec in October, Mudge went on as planned to Niagara, and from there to New York where he rejoined the remainder of the expedition. At the end of 1839 the two commissioners returned to England, and in the following April they submitted a detailed report to Lord Palmerston, the British Foreign Secretary.[1]

As a prelude to their principal conclusion, Featherstonhaugh and Mudge embarked on a lengthy and perhaps gratuitous discussion of the entire history of the eastern boundary, and urged that the western, not the Chiputneticook, branch of the Schoodic should have been selected in 1798 as the stream containing the true source of the St. Croix. Not only did they advocate reopening this old but settled controversy, but they also argued that the North Line of the treaty should in fact run northwest, in a straight line from the source of the St. Croix to a point in the highlands near the source of the Chaudière. This point, in their view, was the true northwest angle. The main assertion of the report, however, is the existence of an uninterrupted line of highlands, described by the authors as an "axis of maximum elevation", running northeasterly from the northwesternmost head of the Connecticut River to the source of the Chaudière and thence to the Baie des Chaleurs. In other words, the commissioners purported to have discovered highlands in the second of the three locations that their instructions had required them to investigate. They also reported no other highlands that would satisfy either the 1783 treaty description or the United States claim. They argued that their own line of highlands was once a continuous ridge, parts of which had become so abraded and broken down by ancient natural causes that the original ridge was nearly obliterated, leaving only peaks at a great distance from each other. More than half of the main report is devoted to a consideration of documentary and other evidence concerning the British and French colonial boundaries before 1783, but the authors do not discuss the existing boundary between New Brunswick and Lower Canada as was requested in their instructions.

As a courtesy, Lord Palmerston transmitted a copy of the Featherstonhaugh-Mudge report to the United States authorities in June 1840, even before it had been introduced in Parliament. It was received by the Americans with predictable anger and denunciation. Governor John Kent, in an address to the Maine legislature in January 1841, poured scorn on Featherstonhaugh's notion that geological processes had abraded antediluvian mountains and turned them into beds of rivers. The earth as it existed in 1783 determined the location of the treaty

---

1 The report contains 88 folio pages of main text and appendix, together with a map. See *British Parliamentary Papers: Colonies, Canadian Boundary*, I, 1831-1840 (Shannon, Ireland, 1969), Correspondence, Part II, pp. 7-57, 1-37.

highlands, he protested, not the "mere speculations of self-styled geologists concerning imaginary or theoretical highlands".[2]   Two months later a joint committee of the same legislature loftily condemned the commissioners' report by speaking of its "impudence, its audacity, and its mendacity; of its sophistries and evasions; of its assumptions, as well as its suppressions; of its profligate perversions, and its presumptuous and extravagant pretensions".[3]

But a more venomous personal attack came from the pen of Charles Francis Adams, a Massachusetts politician and son of the sixth United States president. In an article attributed to him in the *North American Review*, April 1841, he declared Colonel Mudge to be the author of the appendix containing the technical survey data, which in his view was the most useful part of the report, and said that Featherstonhaugh had contributed the remainder.   This unsupported, mean-spirited accusation ignores the commissioners' joint responsibility for their submission. Charging the geologist with having treacherously abused Americans by "studying the surface of their territory at their expense" before accepting the pay of a hostile government, Adams likened Featherstonhaugh to a mercenary knight of the Middle Ages who sold his services to the highest bidder.[4]

Two later commentators have dismissed the value of the controversial report. The Maine historian, J.F. Sprague, writing in 1910 with respect to both the British and the American investigations of 1839-42, concluded that "nothing of impor-tance resulted from either of these surveys".[5] George Classen, a Canadian author, more emphatically declared in 1965 that the Featherstonhaugh-Mudge "report cannot rank as a high point in British survey history.... It had no influence whatever on the boundary settlement".[6] These conclusions are too sweeping and condemnatory. Featherstonhaugh and Mudge were specifically directed to find the line of highlands that corresponded to the 1783 treaty, "Highlands which divide those Rivers that empty themselves into the River St. Lawrence from those which fall into the Atlantic Ocean",[7] and their instructions made it clear that the word "highlands" must be given its ordinary meaning of an elevated or mountain-ous region. It was their attempt to discover those highlands that led the commis-sioners to undertake their extensive topographical and barometric survey, the results of which occupy the 37-page appendix to their report. They adopted the expression "axis of maximum elevation" to describe a chain of highlands which, though formerly continuous, had since become separated in places to form distinct, disconnected peaks. Although their interpretation of a 60-year old treaty on the basis of previous geological action may appear fanciful, it was not

---

2   *Ibid.*, II, 1842-1851, Correspondence 1843, p. 52.

3   *Ibid.*, p. 102.

4   *North American Review*, 52 (April 1841), p.428.

5   J.F. Sprague, *The North Eastern Boundary Controversy and the Aroostook War* (Dover, Maine, 1910), p. 28.

6   H.G. Classen, *Thrust and Counterthrust* (Toronto, 1965), p.71.

7   Hunter Miller, *Treaties and other international acts of the United States of America* (Washington, 1931-48), II, p.152.

implausible, given the cartographic errors and uncertainties that existed when the treaty was signed. Featherstonhaugh and Mudge put forward views that were undoubtedly partisan and drawn from a necessarily rapid field survey. Nevertheless, the information they collected, together with that of the other British and American surveys that followed, contributed toward the eventual appreciation by both sides that topographical data alone could never settle the dispute, and that a conventional boundary would have to be established. From the point of view of the controversy and impact that followed its reception, the Featherstonhaugh and Mudge report remains a milestone in the boundary exploration and evolution. The technical information they gathered, including the map that illustrated their findings, is still of value as a survey record.

The weakness of the British position was apparent as early as 1785 when Sir Guy Carleton, the commander-in-chief, realized that the acceptance of the northern highlands near the St. Lawrence River as the Quebec-New Brunswick boundary would strengthen the American argument that the same highlands defined the 1783 treaty limits.[8] A resolution of the New Brunswick legislature in 1814, calling for an adjustment of the international boundary to permit the important communication with Quebec, was itself a tacit admission of the United States claim.[9] Even Ward Chipman, Sr., the British agent to the boundary commission appointed under Article V of the Treaty of Ghent, had earlier acknowledged that the highlands lay north of the Saint John River, and was obliged to reverse his opinion in 1818 when he argued that Mars Hill was the northwest angle.[10]

But the American contention was also suspect. In its 1829 submission to the king of the Netherlands, the United States claimed that the critical requirement of the controversial treaty feature was that it divided the rivers, and that the word "highlands" by itself was merely of "relative import and indeterminate significacion".[11] Indeed, Albert Gallatin, United States minister to London and one of the authors of the official statements to the royal arbiter, went so far as to argue later that "highlands" meant nothing more than land that was higher than the rivers that flowed through it.[12] Both sides were prepared to change their views from time to time, and the United States was obliged to retreat from an embarrassing assertion made in 1802 by James Sullivan, American agent to the St. Croix Commission, that throughout the disputed area from the St. Lawrence to the Chaudière rivers

8 William F. Ganong, "A Monograph of the Evolution of the Boundaries of the Province of New Brunswick", *Proceedings and Transactions of the Royal Society of Canada*, 2nd series, 7 (1901), Section II, pp. 305-6.

9 *Journal of the House of Assembly for the Province of New Brunswick for the year 1814* (Saint John, 1814), p. 39.

10 *Ganong, op. cit.*, pp. 310-2, 321-5.

11 *Statement on the part of the United States, of the case referred, in pursuance of the Convention of 29th September, 1827, between the said States and Great Britain to His Majesty the King of the Netherlands for his decision thereon* (Washington, 1829), p.9.

12 Albert Gallatin, *The Right of the United States of America to the North-Eastern Boundary claimed by them* (New York, 1840), pp.16, 31.

there was simply a "vast extent of high, flat country" forming an "elevated swamp" and that "there is no such chain of mountains as the plans or maps of the country represent under the appellation of highlands".[13]

Since the shortness of the field season had prevented Featherstonhaugh and Mudge from completing their survey, Lord Palmerston made new arrangements for the work to be continued. In June 1840 he instructed James Featherstonhaugh and Captain William Edward Delves Broughton, R.E. to extend the survey along the North Line to the Mitis River, and thence westward to the Connecticut River. In undertaking this work they were accompanied, among other assistants, by two prominent former members of the previous expedition: John Wilkinson and Corporal McQueen.[14] The work lasted two seasons and the surveyors submitted their final report in February 1842.[15] Meanwhile the United States, which had earlier failed to participate in the proposed Anglo-American exploration of the boundary, sent its own commission in 1840 to gather the topographical information it needed. This commission, which spent three field seasons carefully surveying the area, disproved the continuous "axis of maximum elevation" reported by Featherstonhaugh and Mudge.

The results of these British and American surveys demonstrated beyond rebuttal that the physical conditions of the disputed region would never satisfy the respective British and American territorial claims. Clearly a compromise was called for, and it came just six months after the Featherstonhaugh-Broughton report. Under the Webster-Ashburton treaty of 1842, the two countries finally settled the 60-year old boundary controversy. From the territorial point of view, Maine was the loser, since Britain gained nearly 900 square miles more land than the rejected 1831 arbitration had awarded her. To offset this loss, the United States government paid a monetary compensation to Maine and Massachusetts. The Americans also obtained a favourable adjustment of Quebec's boundary with New York, Vermont and New Hampshire, as well as navigation rights on the Saint John River.

Their North American assignment halted at the end of 1839, the British commissioners resumed their respective careers in England. Mudge remained a lieutenant-colonel in the Royal Engineers and acted as an astronomical adviser to the British-American commission that surveyed and marked the final Maine boundary in 1843-45. He retired from the service in 1850, and thereafter appears to have lived quietly on the country estate until his death four years later. Despite the differences in outlook and temperament that are revealed by their private diaries, which they obviously did not show to each other, Featherstonhaugh and Mudge maintained a cordial relationship after the conclusion of their expedition to the highlands. They exchanged friendly correspondence, and on one occasion

---

13 Thomas C. Amory, *Life of James Sullivan* (Boston, 1859), II, p. 406.

14 McQueen, like Hearnden and McGregor, had received 1s. 0d. a working day during the 1839 expedition and a gratuity of £10 at teh end of it.

15 *British Parliamentary Papers: Colonies, Canadian Boundary*, II, 1842-51, (Shannon, Ireland, 1969), Supplementary Reports 1842, pp. 4-120.

16 Howard Jones, *To the Webster-Ashburton Treaty* (Chapel Hill, 1977).

Featherstonhaugh wrote to Mudge describing a recent visit to his former colleague at Beechwood "where the hours passed in so noiseless and satisfactory a manner, that I feel as if I had awakened from a pleasant dream, not easily forgotten, and not easily renewed.... I rejoice to have had a peep at your domestic happiness".[17]

Featherstonhaugh himself continued working at the Foreign Office where he defended the Webster-Ashburton treaty from the public platform, in newspaper articles, and in a publication *Observations upon the Treaty of Washington*, which appeared in 1843. In the following year he was rewarded for past services with the appointment as British Consul at Le Havre, a post that he occupied until his death at age 86. During this period he published two collections of his travels as a geologist for the United States in the 1830s.

Perhaps the most interesting episode of Featherstonhaugh's diplomatic career occurred during the 1848 revolution in France. In a cloak and dagger incident that narrowly eluded detection by the republican authorities, the indomitable British consul arranged the escape to England of the French king, Louis Philippe, and his queen. To disguise the royal refugee, Featherstonhaugh represented him, with concealed humour, to be his uncle, William Smith.[18] The choice of this seemingly unimaginative name was no accident, for William Smith, the father of English geology, was an old friend whom Featherstonhaugh had last met in April 1839 on the eve of his appointment as boundary commissioner. William Smith died in England on 28 August of that same year, the very day when, 3,000 miles away, Featherstonhaugh and Mudge climbed and recorded the height of Mars Hill, that most contentious mountain, in their search for the highlands.

17 S.R. Flint, *Mudge Memoirs* (Truro, 1883), p. 237.

18 W.H.G. Armytage, "G.W. Featherstonhaugh, F.R.S. 1780-1866, Anglo-American Scientist", *Notes and Records of the Royal Society of London*, 11, 2 (March 1955), pp. 228-35.

APPENDIX

The Commissioners' Instructions[1]

Viscount Palmerston to Colonel Mudge and Mr. Featherstonhaugh.

Gentlemen,   Foreign Office, July 9, 1839.

A NEGOTIATION is now going on between Her Majesty's Government and the Government of the United States of America, for the appointment of a joint Commission of Exploration and Survey, with a view to settle and determine the Boundary line between the British Provinces in North America and the State of Maine.

Recent communications from the United States, however, have shown that it will be impossible that this joint Commission can commence its operations before next year. But Her Majesty's Government are of opinion, that advantage ought to be taken of the present Summer to obtain as accurate a knowledge as possible of the nature and configuration of the territory in dispute; and Her Majesty's Government have therefore determined to send out immediately competent persons to examine and survey that district, to make a report there-upon, and to prepare a map thereof.

I have to inform you that I have selected you for this employment, and I now proceed to give you some general instructions for your guidance. You will proceed in the first instance to Fredericton, and from thence you will take such course as may appear to you best calculated to enable you to make the most of the present season. Her Majesty's Government do not expect you to make any extensive and detailed topographical survey of the country in question, because there is not time in the present season for such a survey; but they wish you to ascertain, by the best means within your power, whether a continuity of Highlands can be satisfactorily traced along a line extending from the sources of the Chaudière to the western end of the Bay of Chaleurs. Her Majesty's Government also wish to have a report upon the character and elevation of the country in that part of the due north line from the source of the St. Croix, which lies between the point where the British Commissioners under the Vth Article of the Treaty of Ghent stopped. You will also report which of the three following lines presents the best defined continuity of Highland range.

---

1 *British Parliamentary Papers: Colonies, Canadian Boundary*, I, 1831-40 (Shannon, Ireland, 1969), Correspondence 1840, Part I, p. 86.

First. The line claimed by the British Commissioners from the source of the Chaudière to Mars Hill.

Second. The line from the source of the Chaudière to the point at which a line drawn from that source to the western extremity of the Bay of Chaleurs, intercepts the due north line.

Thirdly. The line claimed by the Americans from the source of the Chaudière to the point at which they make the due north line end.

You will also report in what degree the country bounded by the due north line and the lines claimed by Great Britain and the United States respectively, can be designated as Highlands in the ordinary sense of the term, assuming that term to mean, as stated in the dictionaries, "an elevated or mountainous region", and not a single ridge of hills.

You will also collect whatever traditional or other information you may be able to obtain, as to the former boundary between the old French colonies and the British colonies, before the year 1783, and as to the present Boundary between New Brunswick and Lower Canada. When you shall have completed your survey, or when the season shall no longer permit you to continue your operations, you will return to England, in order to give such verbal information and explanations as Her Majesty's Government may wish to receive from you upon the objects of your mission, in addition to what may be contained in your official report.

I have to add, in conclusion, that you will be accompanied by a sufficient number of intelligent persons to assist you in this service.

FURTHER READING

ADAMS, Charles Francis, "North American Boundary", *North American Review*, 52 (April 1841), pp. 424-52.

ARMYTAGE, W.H.G., "G.W. Featherstonhaugh, F.R.S.1780-1866, Anglo-American Scientist", *Notes and Records of the Royal Society of London*, 11, 2 (March 1955), pp. 228-35.

BULLER, Charles, "Notes upon the South-western Boundary Line of the British Provinces of Lower Canada and New Brunswick and the United States of America", *Westminster Review*, 34, 1 (June 1840), pp. 202-36.

BURRAGE, Henry S., *Maine in the Northeastern Boundary Controversy* (Portland, 1919).

CLASSEN, H.George, *Thrust and Counterthrust* (Toronto, 1965).

CHIPMAN, Ward Jr., *Remarks upon the disputed points of boundary under the fifth article of the Treaty of Ghent, principally compiled from the statements laid by the Government of Great Britain before the king of the Netherlands, as Arbiter* (Saint John, 1839).

FARIS, John T., *The Romance of the Boundaries* (New York, 1926).

FEATHERSTONHAUGH, George William, *The Republic of Cicero* (New York, 1829).

_____, *The Death of Ugolino* (Philadelphia, 1830).

_____, *Historical Sketch of the negotiations at Paris in 1782* (London, 1842).

_____, *Observations upon the Treaty of Washington* (London, 1843).

_____, *Excursion through the Slave States*, 2 vols. (London, 1844).

_____, *A Canoe Voyage up the Minnay Sotor,* 2 vols. (London, 1847). Reprinted by Minnesota Historical Society (St. Paul, 1970).

FEATHERSTONHAUGH, James D., "Memoir of G.W. Featherstonhaugh", *The American Geologist*, 3, 4 (April 1889), pp. 216-23.

FLINT, Stamford R., *Mudge Memoirs* (Truro, England, 1883).

GANONG, William F., "A Monograph of the Evolution of the Boundaries of the Province of New Brunswick", *Proceedings and Transactions of the Royal Society of Canada*, 2nd series, vol. 7 (1901), Section II, pp. 139-449, vol. 12, (1906), Section II, pp. 151-2.

JAMES, George P.R., *A brief history of the United States boundary question* (London, 1839).

JONES, Howard, *To the Webster-Ashburton Treaty* (Chapel Hill, 1977).

MILLS, Dudley A., "British Diplomacy and Canada: The Ashburton Treaty", *United Empire*, 7, 10 (October 1911), pp. 683-712.

MOORE, John Bassett, *History and Digest of the International Arbitrations to which the United States has been a party* (Washington, 1898), I, chs. 3 and 4.

MUDGE, Richard Z., *Observations on railways, with reference to utility, profit, and the obvious necessity for a national system* (London, 1837).

RICHARDSON, James D., *A compilation of the Messages and Papers of the Presidents* (New York, 1897), IV and V.

SPRAGUE, John F., *The North Eastern Boundary Controversy and the Aroostook War* (Dover, Maine, 1910).

_____, "The North Eastern Boundary Controversy, 1783-1842", in Louis C. Hatch, ed., *Maine: A history* (New York, 1919), I, ch. 10.

WHITE, James, "Boundary Disputes and Treaties" in Adam Shortt and Arthur G. Doughty, eds., *Canada and its Provinces* (Toronto, 1913), VIII, part 3.

WIGHTMAN, George, *A Treatise on Roads, in two parts: Part First, On Surveying and Engineering* (Halifax, 1845).

YULE, Patrick, *Remarks on the disputed northwestern boundary of New Brunswick, bordering on the United States of North America, with an explanatory sketch* (2nd ed., London, 1838).

INDEX

DATE DUE

	261-2500		Printed in USA